YORK NOTE

# A Passage to India

## E.M. Forster

### Notes by Nigel Messenger

Longman    York Press

The publishers wish to thank The Provost and Scholars of King's College, Cambridge, and The Society of Authors as the literary representatives of the E.M. Forster Estate.

The right of Nigel Messenger to be identified as Author of this Work has been asserted by him in accordance with the Copyright, Designs and Patents Act 1988

YORK PRESS
322 Old Brompton Road, London SW5 9JH

PEARSON EDUCATION LIMITED
Edinburgh Gate, Harlow,
Essex CM20 2JE, United Kingdom
Associated companies, branches and representatives throughout the world

First published 1999
Fourth impression 2004

ISBN 0-582-41462-8

Designed by Vicki Pacey, Trojan Horse, London
Map artwork by Neil Gower
Phototypeset by Gem Graphics, Trenance, Mawgan Porth, Cornwall
Colour reproduction and film output by Spectrum Colour
Produced by Pearson Education Asia Limited, Hong Kong

# CONTENTS

PART ONE

# INTRODUCTION

## HOW TO STUDY A NOVEL

Studying a novel on your own requires self-discipline and a carefully thought-out work plan in order to be effective.

- You will need to read the novel more than once. Start by reading it quickly for pleasure, then read it slowly and thoroughly.
- On your second reading make detailed notes on the plot, characters and themes of the novel. Further readings will generate new ideas and help you to memorise the details of the story.
- Some of the characters will develop as the plot unfolds. How do your responses towards them change during the course of the novel?
- Think about how the novel is narrated. From whose point of view are events described?
- A novel may or may not present events chronologically: the time-scheme may be a key to its structure and organisation.
- What part do the settings play in the novel?
- Are words, images or incidents repeated so as to give the work a pattern? Do such patterns help you to understand the novel's themes?
- Identify what styles of language are used in the novel.
- What is the effect of the novel's ending? Is the action completed and closed, or left incomplete and open?
- Does the novel present a moral and just world?
- Cite exact sources for all quotations, whether from the text itself or from critical commentaries. Wherever possible find your own examples from the novel to back up your opinions.
- Always express your ideas in your own words.

This York Note offers an introduction to *A Passage to India* and cannot substitute for close reading of the text and the study of secondary sources.

*A Passage to India* is a novel with an unsolved mystery at its centre. What *does* happen to Adela in the cave? There have been many explanations but none quite satisfy; even E.M. Forster admitted in a letter to his friend William Plomer that: 'When asked what happened there, *I don't know*'. Yet readers have been constantly drawn to this novel, will read and re-read it, in an attempt to make some sense to the enigma of the menacing Marabar Hills and their 'extraordinary' caves. Their reverberating 'bou-oum' or 'ou-boum' (Chapter 14, pp. 144–6), the echoes that threaten meaning and overturn reason, continue to excite and exercise our imagination.

In his own critical book on novels and novel writing, *Aspects of the Novel* (1927), E.M. Forster disparaged the capacity of the novel to tell stories, but this novel tells an excellent story. We get all the traditional satisfaction of a well-made plot and solid characterisation too. We not only want to read on because of a strong narrative, we expect, and get, the pleasurable recognition of instantly recognisable English 'types' like Major Callendar and the Turtons, Ronny, whose religion 'was of the sterilized public-school brand, which never goes bad, even in the tropics' (Chapter 28, p. 234) or the witless Mrs Blakiston who dares not return to her bungalow in case the 'niggers attacked' (Chapter 20, p. 172). We are comfortable with comedy and satire of this kind; it draws its security and strength from the social confidence of Jane Austen and the moral severity of George Eliot.

But these traditional pleasures and expectations are subtly qualified by a more oblique and reflexive mode of writing. We are not allowed to lose ourselves in an escapist world. We are always reminded that we are reading a constructed fiction with its own formal structures and modes of organisation. The echoes of the Marabar Caves that torment Adela and Mrs Moore are the most obvious of many reverberations that wash through the text teasing characters and readers alike. *A Passage to India* is a poetic novel that is not afraid to question the efficiency of language or the power of literature to give meaning to a possibly meaningless existence. E.M. Forster queries the place of mankind in the universe as well as question, in a more limited political sense, the destructive presence and injustice of the British in India.

E.M. Forster's philosophy has sometimes been attacked for its rather cosy, dated certitudes but Adela's 'awfully British' honesty

(Chapter 8, p. 91) or Fielding's generous concern for good personal relations seem very inadequate in the mysterious or downright threatening environment of colonial India. E.M. Forster is not afraid in this, his greatest fiction, to expose the limitations of tolerance, sympathy and fair play, those humane nineteenth-century liberal values, in a hostile, divided modern world.

Yet this novel still manages to resist a simple, cynical pessimism and leaves room for the aspirations of the human spirit. As Godbole hopefully consoles himself after his foiled attempt to reach out for the infinite in the last, strange section of this novel: 'One old Englishwoman and one little, little wasp ... It does not seem much, still, it is more than I am myself' (Chapter 33, p. 263).

# PART TWO

# SUMMARIES & COMMENTARIES

E.M. Forster began his last completed novel, *A Passage to India*, after his first visit to India in 1912–13. However, he ran into difficulties with the novel and abandoned it around the present Chapter 14 sometime in 1914. The problem seems to have been his difficulty on deciding on the nature of the fateful events in the Marabar Caves. In one early draft, it is Fielding who experiences the mysterious echo; in another, Aziz and Adela are in the cave together. In one fascinating fragment of manuscript, Adela is actually attacked by an unnamed assailant and beats him off with Ronny's binoculars.

The novel remained unfinished for ten years. In 1921–2, E.M. Forster visited India for a second time and worked as a secretary to the Maharajah of Dewas State Senior for several months. His experiences there provided material for the final section of the novel and refreshed his general sense of the complexities of Indian life at a time of gathering social unrest on the sub-continent. Encouraged by Leonard Woolf, husband of E.M. Forster's fellow Bloomsbury novelist Virginia Woolf, E.M. Forster seems to have completed the novel early in 1924. It was first published by Edward Arnold later that year.

The definitive edition of the novel is Volume Six of the Collected Abinger edition of E.M. Forster's works published by Edward Arnold and edited by Oliver Stallybrass in 1979. For the advanced student, an accompanying volume in the Abinger edition gives all the known manuscript variations and rejected drafts. The modern Penguin edition (1979) is reset from the Abinger text with the original preface by Stallybrass, appendices and full notes, some by E.M. Forster himself. It also has a glossary of unfamiliar Indian vocabulary. This is the best edition for students and my page references refer to this text.

The novel is set during the British Raj. Chandrapore is a town on the Ganges in north-eastern India. It is without interest save for the Marabar Hills and their extraordinary caves that lie twenty miles away. Adela Quested accompanies Mrs Moore on a visit to Chandrapore to see her son, the new City Magistrate, Ronny Heaslop. Adela and Ronny have met in England and the primary purpose of the visit is to confirm an engagement between the young couple. Adela is a serious-minded girl who wants to see 'the *real* India'. While she is at the English Club expressing this wish, Mrs Moore meets a young Moslem, Dr Aziz, by chance, in a small mosque on a evening walk by herself. Aziz is proud and sensitive; a social evening with his friends has just been disrupted by an imperious summons by his superior at the City Hospital, Major Callendar, and a snub by his wife. He is angry at first, but, when he sees that Mrs Moore respects his religion, an intimacy quickly develops between them. To please Adela, the Collector, Mr Turton, arranges a Bridge Party, where the English visitors can meet some local Indians at the club. This is not a success, but the women meet Cyril Fielding, the Principal of the Government College. He likes their liberal attitude and invites them to tea at the college along with the Hindu Brahmin, Professor Godbole, and Dr Aziz. He has wanted to meet Aziz for some time and the feeling is mutual. Aziz arrives early and they immediately establish a friendly rapport. The tea-party starts well and Aziz impetuously invites the English ladies on an expedition to visit the Marabar Hills and their famous caves. However, Ronny arrives, is displeased by the lax informality of the gathering and the party breaks up in some discomfort. Adela considers that Anglo-Indian life has changed Ronny for the worse and decides that she cannot marry him, but a mysterious car accident brings them together again. The first section ends with Adela and Ronny now formally engaged, and Fielding and Aziz firm friends.

The ill-fated expedition to the Marabar Caves coincides with the arrival of the hot weather. Matters do not go smoothly from the start as Fielding and Godbole miss the train. Despite Aziz's costly and elaborate preparations, the visit proves to be a disappointment. On entering the first cave, Mrs Moore becomes ill. She suffers from claustrophobia and also from a strange spiritual disillusionment caused by the cave's empty echo. Apart from a single guide, Adela and Aziz go on alone. They become separated and enter different caves. The guide loses Adela and Aziz next sees her at the foot of the hills talking to an English woman, Miss Derek. They drive away. Aziz arrives back at the camp to find that Fielding has arrived in Miss Derek's car. He is so pleased that he makes light of Adela's strange behaviour. On their return to Chandrapore, Aziz is arrested for molesting Adela in a cave. In an atmosphere of hysteria and racial mistrust, attitudes soon harden between the British and Indian communities. Fielding believes that Aziz has been falsely accused and resigns from the English Club. Adela has suffered a breakdown complaining of a strange echo in her head. Mrs Moore also acts strangely; she too believes Aziz to be innocent, but takes no further interest in the proceedings and soon leaves India for home. On the day of the trial, she dies at sea, but Indians outside the court chant her name believing she would testify for the defence if she could. Inside, Adela is led through the events of the fateful day and suddenly declares Aziz to be innocent. The trial breaks-up in disorder, Adela is disowned by the Anglo-Indian community and is protected by Fielding much to the displeasure of Aziz and his Indian friends. Adela and Fielding grow to like and respect each other, but cannot make any sense of the events at the Marabar Hills. Ronny breaks off the engagement and Adela leaves for home. Aziz is suspicious that Fielding plans to marry Adela himself and has persuaded him to forgo his rightful compensation for that reason. He is deliberately absent from Chandrapore when Fielding, too, departs for leave in England.

The final section of the novel takes place at Mau, a Hindu native state in central India, two years later. Godbole is Minister for Education and, through his influence, Aziz is now the personal physician of the Maharajah. It is the time of the monsoon and the climax of the Gokul Ashtami festivities celebrating the birth of Krishna. Godbole remembers Mrs Moore in a trance-like state as he leads the religious worship. Aziz learns of Fielding's arrival on an official visit as an Education Inspector with his wife and her brother. Believing that Fielding has married Adela, he has no wish to meet him. When they do meet at a small Moslem shrine, he discovers that it is not Adela that Fielding has married but Stella, Mrs Moore's daughter by her second marriage and half-sister of Ronny Heaslop. Later that evening, he visits the State Guest House to attend Ralph Moore who has been stung by bees. He finds himself

---

strangely drawn to him, just as he was to his mother. They row out onto the great Mau tank to see the final torchlight procession of Gokul Ashtami. Fielding and Stella are also in a boat which collides with them, capsizing everyone together into the water at the conclusion of the festival. This accident heals the breach between the two friends but, as they go riding the following day, they recognise they cannot sustain true friendship while political inequality exists between their two nations. Despite their private feelings for each other, the Indian earth and sky will always intervene to cry 'No, not yet', and 'No, not there' (Chapter 37, p. 289).

# DETAILED SUMMARIES

## PART 1: MOSQUE

CHAPTER 1     **An introduction to Chandrapore. Two contrasting views. The overarching sky and the extraordinary caves**

The novel opens with a short description of Chandrapore and an overview of the surrounding countryside. We first gain an impression of the town as filthy and nondescript from ground level. The perspective is from the street and the river Ganges which flows past the native quarter. Then the view shifts to the elevated vantage point of the European civil station. This has nothing to recommend it either but it has a view of the town below which is quite different: from this position Chandrapore seems beautiful and fertile. Finally the **omniscient narrator** contemplates the vastness of the Indian sky and the 'fists and fingers' of the Marabar Hills that thrust up through the monotony of the Indian plain.

> The novel is divided into three major sections, each introduced by a brief introductory chapter. These set up a perspective from which to view the succeeding events in the section and anticipate the dominant themes and issues of each one through suggestive **imagery**. Hence this chapter should be compared with Chapter 12 and Chapter 33 (See Narrative Techniques and Structure). The tone here is of the detached European traveller writing a travelogue that expresses a bemused fascination with the scale, strangeness and deceptive qualities of the Indian landscape. This is appropriate for

much in the 'Mosque' section that follows will illustrate India's power to charm and confuse. The two contradictory views that we have of Chandrapore from below and above stress the divided nature of Indian society and hence the perceptions of different racial groups from the outset. The chapter ends with a reference to the 'fists and fingers' of the Marabar Hills suggesting their importance in the subsequent narrative.

Chandrapore is based on the Indian town of Bankipore near Patna which E.M. Forster visited on his first trip to India in 1912–13.

**maidan**   large park or public space

**Eurasians**   people of mixed European and Asian descent

**neem trees**   common Indian trees

**peepul**   a large tree with long leaves

**tanks**   lakes or reservoirs of water

**Civil Station**   an area reserved for European residence

CHAPTER 2    **Dr Aziz visits his friend Hamidullah. The impossibility of friendship with an Englishman. A summons and a snub. Aziz meets Mrs Moore in the mosque. 'The secret understanding of the heart!' (p. 38)**

The perspective now shifts and focuses on Aziz, an educated Moslem doctor, as he spends an evening in the native quarter with his friends. Waiting for dinner they debate the impossibility of ever finding true friendship with any of their colonial masters because, once in India, Englishmen and women soon become arrogant and suspicious. We learn that Aziz is a widower with three small children to support but he is reluctant to marry again. The social gathering is disrupted when he is ordered to go to Major Callendar's bungalow. He arrives to find Callendar gone without explanation. His greeting to Mrs Callendar and her friend is ignored as they take his carriage, leaving him to walk back to the native quarter. Resting in a small mosque, Aziz dreams of Islamic poetry and lost Islamic power when he is disturbed by an elderly English woman. His initial hostility is disarmed when he discovers that she is respectful of his religious beliefs. They talk of children, domestic matters and his grievances as he escorts her back to the English Club which he cannot enter.

E.M. Forster opens up the theme of mutual suspicion and division between the races in India from the perspective of the Moslem community. We get a sense of Aziz's pride in the poetry of Islam and its cultural legacy. This chapter is set in the evening as are many of the scenes in the 'Mosque' section which emphasise the mystery and beauty of India. The interrupted social gathering is one of several in this first section which emphasises the fragility of all social connections and so becomes a **motif** in E.M. Forster's narrative patterning (see Chapters 7, 16 and the section on 'rhythm' under Narrative Techniques and Structure). Aziz's social unease and insensitive treatment at the hands of the Callendars confirm the truth of the earlier conversation, but this is surprisingly qualified by the unexpected meeting of minds in the mosque. An elderly English woman and a young Indian man find a strange affinity in a quiet space between the two communities. 'Then you are an Oriental' (p. 41), Aziz's tribute to Mrs Moore, will return to haunt him in the final stages of the novel (see Chapter 36, p. 280).

**champak**  Indian tree with scented flowers
**Hafiz**  Persian poet of the fourteenth century (1320–89)
**Hali**  Urdu poet and critic (1837–1914)
**Iqbal**  Urdu poet and philosopher (1875–1938)
**chuprassy**  porter
**tonga**  horse carriage
**Huzoor**  polite form of address
**Deccan**  the south of India
*Cousin Kate*  a popular Edwardian play
**Civil Surgeon**  government medical doctor responsible for a district hospital

CHAPTER 3    **The English Club. Adela Quested's wish 'to see the** ***real*** **India' (p. 42). English attitudes towards the Indians. Mrs Moore and Ronny Heaslop. Mrs Moore and the wasp**

The scene now shifts to the Anglo-English community and their prejudices and hostilities. The theme of exclusion and inclusion is developed as we learn from the Turtons that Ronny Heaslop is a 'sahib' and 'one of us' but that Fielding is not 'pukka'. Adela's wish to meet 'real Indians' is indulged. Turton agrees to organise a 'Bridge Party' to help West meet East. We learn (p. 46) of Ronny's reason for his treatment of Mahmoud Ali (see p. 31) which is challenged by Adela. He is further discomforted by his mother's meeting with Aziz and seeks to find reasons to discourage such encounters which Mrs Moore resists. The chapter ends on a poetical note as she meditates upon a wasp sleeping on a peg in her bedroom.

There is much social **satire** in this chapter as the **omniscient narrator** makes fun of the insular habits of the English: the barred windows, the amateur dramatics, the semi-religious ritual of the National Anthem. The cynicism and sourness of the Anglo-Indian community is contrasted with the fresh openness of the visiting Mrs Moore and Adela Quested. Ronny has already been changed by the atmosphere as his guests seem to recognise. The mood lifts when they move outside and become conscious of the moon's splendour reflected in the water of the Ganges. This links with the references to poetry and the beauty of the Indian night in Chapter 2. This chapter ends on a note of mystical sympathy as Mrs Moore contemplates the sleeping wasp ('Pretty dear' p. 50) which knows of no barriers or exclusions. The wasp is a **motif** associated with Mrs Moore which will reappear at the end of the novel (see Chapter 33, p. 259).

> **memsahibs** wives of British officials
>
> **Collector** term for the chief administrator of an Indian district
>
> **Burra Sahib** the great master
>
> **Vakil** barrister
>
> **izzat** reputation
>
> **Aryan brother** the Collector refers, sarcastically, to the nineteenth-century racial and linguistic theory that maintained the races of Western Europe and Northern India shared a common ancestral stock from Southern Russia called Aryans

CHAPTER 4    **Invitations**

This short chapter explores the effect of the Collector's invitations to a Bridge Party on the local community. It ends with more general philosophical speculation on the nature of inclusion and exclusion.

The reception of the invitation reveals tension and suspicion, not only towards the British community but among the Indians themselves. The final paragraph is rich with **irony** as the **omniscient narrator** explores the **theme** of invitations which is so evident in this first section (see Chapters 3, 5, 6, 7). To invite some people is always to exclude others; comprehensive unity seems impossible to achieve. Even the Christian God of old Mr Graysford and young Mr Sorley seems inadequate to the challenge of an all-inclusive acceptance of all material things.

**Nawab**  a Moslem prince

CHAPTER 5    **The Bridge Party. Fielding's invitation to Adela. Mrs Moore discusses the English in India with Ronny**

The 'Bridge Party' is not a success. The Indians are socially constrained and the English are arrogant. Mrs Moore and Adela do their best to meet Indians despite Mrs Turton's disdain and the Principal of the Government College, Mr Fielding, also mixes freely. There is a bungled, confused attempt by Mrs Moore to arrange a further meeting with Mrs Bhattacharya and Fielding, pleased with the visitors' attempts at sociability, invites the ladies to tea to meet some Indians. Adela has a depressing vision of what her life would be as the wife of an Anglo-Indian official. Later Mrs Moore and Ronny talk about life in India. Ronny is angered by his mother's implied criticism of the behaviour of Anglo-Indians and gives a rather clichéd, self-pitying defence. She gives an impassioned plea for more Christian love and charity in India while feeling the inadequacy of her religious feelings. The chapter ends with the unresolved question that has brought her to India: will Adela and Ronny marry?

The 'Bridge Party' and Ronny's pompous self-justifications allow the narrator ample scope to exercise his talent for comedy and **satirical** commentary. For example, it is evident that Mrs Turton is less well educated and travelled than the Indian ladies she patronises. But not all is satire. The exchange between Mrs Bhattacharya and the visitors demonstrates the difficulties of crossing a cultural divide, even when goodwill exists on both sides. The **motif** of the 'overarching sky' in Chapter 1, is repeated here

(p. 55) and puts the littleness of the Anglo-Indians and their preoccupations into a much wider perspective. Also, in the final paragraph Mrs Moore seems to sense the limitation and inadequacy of western Christianity in India which has been suggested already at the end of Chapter 4. Her tentative assertion 'God … is … love' (p. 64) will reappear strangely transposed much later in the novel as 'God si Love' (see Chapter 33, p. 258).

**Pathan**  member of warlike tribe on North-West Frontier

***Quality Street***  play (1902) by James Barrie (1860–1937)

**Parsee**  member of an ancient religious sect

**bhang**  an intoxicant

**P.–and–O.**  the Peninsular and Oriental Steam Navigation Company which operated the route between London and Bombay

**the hills**  the hill stations in Northern India

CHAPTER 6    **Aziz mourns his wife and upsets Dr Panna Lal. Polo with the subaltern and an invitation from Fielding**

The focus shifts back to Aziz who did not attend the Bridge Party because of the anniversary of his wife's death. He is unreasonably rebuked by his superior, Major Callendar, for his failure to respond soon enough to his order but the Major knows that Aziz is a more skilful surgeon than he is. Aziz had agreed to attend the Bridge Party with Dr Panna Lal, but makes his excuses which are not accepted. He mourns sincerely over the photograph of his dead wife and then practices polo in the Maidan before returning home to discover an invitation from Fielding.

This chapter continues to explore how our relationships are determined by external factors. Aziz's experience shows that genuine love can grow from the structure of an arranged marriage. His grief is sincere and religion offers little consolation for the loss of his wife. Two encounters show the part that chance and prejudice often play. Because Dr Panna Lal is Hindu, a cultural antipathy exacerbates the personal friction over Aziz's failure to attend the Bridge Party, and the good feeling between Aziz and the subaltern is only a temporary truce between different cultures as both men are both caught up in the pleasure of physical exercise. The subaltern will reappear in Chapter 20 (pp. 174–5) where this episode gets a more **ironic** treatment.

**chukker**  round of polo

CHAPTER 7     **Introducing Fielding. His first meeting with Aziz. The tea-party with Mrs Moore, Adela and Professor Godbole. Aziz's invitation to the Marabar Caves. Ronny's interruption and Godbole's invitation to God**

Fielding is a liberal, broad-minded man who has travelled widely and does not fit into the narrow world of the Anglo-Indian club. He is popular with his pupils but not with the English community, especially the women, so he lives an independent life. Despite some cultural misunderstandings, Fielding and Aziz take to each other immediately and Aziz gives Fielding his collar-stud when he breaks his own. Fielding lives in a Moslem garden-house so Aziz is able to relax and indulge his dreams of Islamic culture and power. Initially the meeting with Fielding's other guests is a great success. The ladies are puzzled by the failure of the Bhattacharyas to send their carriage, and, rashly, Aziz seeks to remedy this failure of hospitality by inviting them on an excursion to the Marabar Caves. Aziz has never visited the caves himself, and Professor Godbole is enigmatic when asked why they are considered extraordinary. Fielding and Mrs Moore are touring the college when Ronny arrives. He is very displeased to find Adela unchaperoned by Europeans and the party breaks up in some discord and bad temper, but not before Godbole has sung a raga begging Shri Krishna to come to earth but he refuses. Mrs Moore asks if he comes in some other song. Godbole says no: he 'neglects to come' (p. 87).

> This chapter is pivotal to the 'Mosque' section of the novel and moves the action forward significantly. The initial meeting between Aziz and Fielding can be compared with that between Aziz and Mrs Moore (Chapter 2). Both occur in marginal spaces, one public, one domestic, both expressive of the generous Islamic spirit of hospitality. The description of a social gathering interrupted and broken-up is one that we have already encountered in Chapter 2 so this is a good example of what E.M. Forster himself called 'rhythm'

(see Language and Style). Two important **themes** are developed here. One is that of invitations. Aziz invites the ladies to visit the Marabar Caves, Godbole invites Shri Krishna to earth. The failure of the latter casts an ominous shadow on the former. Ronny also brings an invitation, a coercive invitation to a polo match that takes the ladies away from their host. The other is the theme of India as 'mystery' or 'muddle'. Which is it? The question will reverberate through the novel (see especially Chapters 8, 19, 33 and also Recurring Themes). Apart from Aziz's impulsive invitation, the action is significantly developed by Adela's unguarded admission that she does not intend to stay in India.

**Loggia de' Lanzi**  a public square in Florence

**Maude Goodman**  minor painter

**dhoti**  loin-cloth

**Elephanta**  beautiful caves near Bombay

**Siva**  Hindu god

**Parvati**  Hindu goddess, wife of Siva

CHAPTER 8    **Adela rejects Ronny but later changes her mind and they become engaged. The ride and mysterious accident in the Nawab Bahadur's car. Thoughts of ghosts in the Indian night**

Ronny and Adela are in a bad humour with each other and Mrs Moore is tired of them both. They leave her at the bungalow and go to the polo match where Adela declares that she cannot marry Ronny. He accepts her decision with some dignity and they feel a sense of lonely camaraderie in a strange country far from home. The Nawab Bahadur invites them for a drive in his car. There is an accident when the car is hit by a mysterious animal. Miss Derek arrives on the scene and takes the English couple and the Nawab back to Chandrapore. In the general excitement, Adela and Ronny have drawn together again and announce their engagement to Mrs Moore on their return. She is oddly disturbed by the accident and has a premonition of ghosts. Down in Chandrapore, the Nawab Bahadur tells the story of a past accident when a man was killed by his car. He is convinced that the accident was caused by the spirit of the man waiting at the spot to avenge his death.

Adela and Ronny drift into an engagement rather than make a deliberate decision. It is a choice of the known in an India full of the unknown like the unidentified little green bird (pp. 91–2). The accident is an intervention from a world of mystery or muddle that brings them together fortuitously. Mrs Moore seems to be in tune with this world because her sense of supernatural events is confirmed by the Nawab's story. We see that Ronny consistently misjudges or misunderstands the behaviour of the Indians he meets because he doesn't know all the facts, either the reason why the Nawab panics or why Aziz is lacking a collar-stud. The incident on the Marabar road anticipates the much more dramatic and dreadful experience in the Marabar Caves later (see Chapters 14–16).

**topi** hat or cap

**peon** servant

CHAPTER 9    **Goodwill and conflict by Aziz's sickbed**

Aziz has a mild fever and takes to his bed in his shabby, flyblown bungalow. Pretending to be worse than he is, he dreams of a discreet but disreputable bachelor trip to Calcutta. Various sets of visitors arrive to see him. First his Moslem friends, Hamidullah, Mr Haq, and Syed Mohammed with his nephew Rafi. Aziz is concerned that Professor Godbole is also ill. Rafi suggests that it is suspicious that both of them were at Fielding's tea-party but this thought is quickly repressed as unworthy. However, the conversation soon moves on to denounce the unhygienic nature of Hindus generally and to celebrate Moslem culture. The mood is broken by Dr Panna Lal and Ram Chand, who arrive to ascertain the state of Aziz's health for Major Callendar. Very soon a quarrel breaks out between the Hindus and Moslems that is interrupted by the arrival of Fielding. He too is drawn into a political debate about atheism and the moral right of the British to rule India. He leaves with the others feeling his visit has been a failure.

E.M. Forster uses social comedy to illustrate ethnic tensions among the Indians themselves. Moslem aspirations towards beauty and unity compare with the Hindu call to Krishna at the end of Chapter 7 (p. 87); like Krishna, the ideal Friend never comes, 'yet is not entirely disproved' (p. 108). We are alerted to the barriers of language by Rafi's feeble excuse for his malicious gossip (p. 110) and by the reception of Fielding's rational conversation (p. 113). Hamidullah is moved to think that England has 'sufficient substructure for a national life' but here 'all was wire-pulling and fear' (p. 108). Fielding's thought that the Club would consider his behaviour 'cheap' echoes Ram Chand's warning to the Nawab Bahadur in Chapter 4 (p. 51). Everywhere in India suspicion threatens hospitality and human contact.

**Ghalib** Urdu and Persian poet (1796–1869)
**Jain** Jainism is an ancient religion from around 500 BC

CHAPTER 10    The arrival of the hot weather

This is a short meditative chapter similar to Chapter 4 where the **omniscient narrator** considers the self-defeating power of the sun as it rules India with more authority than the British. Its power is absolute yet it is 'debarred from glory' (p. 116) because it can only divide people never unite them. This chapter prepares the reader for the heat of the Indian summer which dominates the visit to the Marabar Caves and its aftermath in the next section.

CHAPTER 11    Aziz and Fielding consolidate their friendship

Fielding is about to depart when Aziz calls him back. As an expression of his friendship, he shows the Englishman a photograph of his dead wife, a magnanimous gesture and a very great complement. He declares that India can only be united by kindness and feelings not on bureaucracy and political reforms. Aziz's emotional generosity overwhelms Fielding and makes him conscious of his inadequacies. He travels light with no commitments or family. He believes in individuals and, unlike Aziz, he has no roots in society. Aziz believes him to be reckless in his unguarded conversation, but, soothed by the development of their intimacy, drifts into sleep dreaming of past Moslem glory.

This chapter concludes the first section of the novel on an appropriate note of qualified harmony. Adela and Ronny are engaged and Aziz and Fielding are now firm friends. The personal life has triumphed. But for how long? Even at this moment of intimate friendship, Fielding finds Aziz's references to Adela's breasts in poor taste, and Aziz patronises Fielding's lack of guile. From what we have learned in this first section, Aziz's demand for 'Kindness, more kindness, and even after that more kindness' (p. 118) in India seems a forlorn hope indeed.

**saddhus** Hindu religious ascetics

## PART 2: CAVES

### CHAPTER 12   A description of the Marabar Caves

As in the 'Mosque' section, the second part of the novel opens with an introductory chapter (see Chapters 1 and 33). As before, the style and tone are of a travelogue as an urbane, European sensibility engages with the strangeness of the Indian landscape. If the moon was a dominant **motif** in the 'Mosque' section, it is the sun here. The Marabar Hills are 'flesh of the sun's flesh' and of 'incredible antiquity' (p. 125). unmarked by man's religions, they are 'Extraordinary' yet contain 'Nothing' (p. 126).

The description of the caves here emphasises their imperviousness to human interpretation and their resistance to meaning. They are both monotonous and beautiful. 'They are like nothing else in the world' (p. 125). The writing achieves great **lyric** force as the narrator describes the flames' reflection on the polished inner surface of the caves. The flames are seen as fragile human interventions from the outside that briefly bring beauty and illumination but are doomed to extinction (compare the 'Little ineffectual unquenchable flames' of human goodwill in Chapter 9, p. 109); the infinite regress of the mirrored darkness of the Kawa Dol (p. 127) is an internal counterpart to the 'overarching sky' of the opening chapter (p. 30). Describing the hills as thrusting up like 'Fists and fingers' through the 'advancing soil' and the internal surface of the caves as 'skin, finer than any covering acquired by the animals' (p. 126), E.M. Forster is using **anthropomorphism** for suggestive, poetic effect. The instability of the boulder on the Kawa Dol ends the chapter on a menacing note.

The Marabar Hills are based on the Barabar Hills that E.M. Forster visited on his first Indian trip in 1913. They are more dispersed than E.M. Forster's fictional hills and not visible from Bankipore (the model for E.M. Forster's Chandrapore); there are also fewer caves than E.M. Forster suggests.

**Vishnu** the second member of the Hindu Trinity, Brahma, Vishnu and Siva. He is called the Preserver

**Siva's hair** Siva, the third Hindu god, is the Destroyer and Restorer

**Dravidia** Southern India

CHAPTER 13    **Preparations for the expedition to the Marabar Caves. Chaos at the station. Fielding and Professor Godbole miss the train**

Although Aziz regrets his rash invitation, and no-one is enthusiastic, the visit to the caves is to go ahead despite difficulties and inconvenience. Aziz makes elaborate preparations and stays overnight at the station to avoid unpunctuality. In the event, it is Fielding who misses the train, delayed by Godbole's prayers, and the English ladies leave unaccompanied by their own servant.

Aziz has 'challenged the spirit of the Indian earth, which tries to keep men in compartments' (p. 129). He tries to sustain the spirit of Moslem hospitality despite the restraints and restrictions imposed by the varied racial and religious composition of the party. Although there is much incidental comedy as the party boards the train, the absence of Fielding introduces an element of anxiety into the disorder of the train's departure for the caves. Also the bribing of Anthony, the Englishwomen's servant, to stay behind seems harmless enough and done to satisfy Adela as much as appease Aziz, but, like Fielding's lateness, ominous significance will be made of it later.

**Brahman** member of a priestly Hindu caste

**pujah** religious ceremony

CHAPTER 14   The train journey to the Marabar Hills. The false
             dawn. An elephant ride and more hospitality on their
             arrival. The party visits the first cave. Mrs Moore's
             unpleasant and negative experience. Aziz, Adela and
             a guide go on to the Kawa Dol

The two English women are experiencing a growing apathy in India.
During the journey, Adela discusses her future but Mrs Moore can
only feel a disillusionment with marriage generally. This mood of
disenchantment extends to the Indian landscape which resists any
attempt to interpret it. The dawn promises much but proves to be
disappointing and their destination is 'A horrid, stuffy place' (p. 140).
Aziz seeks to revive a mood of romance with his talk of the great
Moslem rulers of India and his lavish provision of an elephant, but his
pleasure in giving hospitality is quickly dispelled when Adela begins to
discuss the problems of being an Anglo-Indian. During their visit to the
first cave, Mrs Moore experiences panic and claustrophobia. She is also
upset by the terrifying echo in the cave. It begins to 'undermine her hold
on life' (p. 146) and her Christian faith. Resting at the camp while the
others go on, this negative experience of meaninglessness is of such
power that she loses the will to communicate with her children or anyone
else.

Adela has wanted to see the 'real' India but this chapter shows
how difficult a project this is. For the European trained to expect
coherence and logic, the Indian landscape is an alien, baffling
place. 'How can the mind take hold of such a country' (p. 136).
Even Aziz has to admit that 'Nothing embraces the whole of India,
nothing, nothing ...' (p. 142). The dawn refuses to give the
expected romantic thrill for India is not 'manageable' like Grasmere
(p. 137) and a snake proves to be a tree stump after all (p. 139).
Adela is concerned that she cannot escape the 'label' and maybe
the conditioning of being Anglo-Indian, but the Marabar Hills
remain primeval, anterior to all labelling. Mrs Moore's crisis in
the cave is a crucial development in the novel. Her panic
anticipates Adela's later, but is more fully explained. The physical
alarm she feels is shown to be needless when she recovers and
looks around her but the echoing 'bou-oum' or 'ou-boum' is a

different matter. It represents a challenge to language, the means by which we communicate with each other. By undermining language, the echo threatens all the ways by which human beings impose culture and hence meaning upon the world and their experience of the world. Mrs Moore's religion is 'poor little talkative Christianity' (p. 146) and it proves inadequate to the nihilistic message of the caves that the universe is indifferent to us: 'Everything exists, nothing has value' (p. 146).

**Taj** the Taj Mahal, built at Agra

**the goddess Parvati** Hindu goddess, wife of Siva

**Emperor Babur** first Mogul Emperor (1483–1530)

**Aurangzebe** last of the great Moguls (1618–1707)

**Akbar** Mogul Emperor (1542–1605)

CHAPTER 15   **Adela and Aziz climb to the Kawa Dol preoccupied with their own thoughts. Adela innocently offends Aziz with a tactless remark. They go into different caves**

Aziz worries about the adequacy of his breakfast preparations while Adela considers her wedding and future as the wife of an Anglo-Indian official. As she looks at some footholds in the rock, she is reminded of the incident with the Nawab Bahadur's car (Chapter 8) and suddenly realises that she does not love Ronny. With love and marriage on her mind, she asks Aziz if he is married and whether he has more than one wife. Aziz is shocked and goes into a cave to cover his embarrassment. Adela wanders into another still thinking about marriage.

Adela tries to plan her future conscientiously. The hot stony landscape seems to be an expression of her rather barren common sense as she confronts the thought of a loveless marriage and feels 'vexed rather than appalled' (p. 148). Her curiosity about Aziz is already coloured by the condescending, patronising attitudes of Anglo-India.

chapter 16   **Arrival of Fielding and the sudden, unexplained departure of Adela with Miss Derek. The return of the party to Chandrapore and Aziz's arrest at the station**

When Aziz comes out of the cave, he is disturbed to find Adela has disappeared. The guide has lost her and runs away. He begins to panic but then sees her talking to someone by a car at the foot of the hills. They drive away. Aziz picks up Adela's field-glasses with the strap broken at the mouth of one of the caves and returns to the camp to find Fielding has arrived. Miss Derek has brought him but he is surprised to discover that she has already gone back to Chandrapore with Adela. He fears that something is amiss but Aziz, delighted at the unexpected arrival of his friend, makes light of the matter and invents some polite fictions to excuse her. On their return to Chandrapore, they find the police are waiting for Aziz at the station. Fielding manages to stop him resisting arrest.

> In terms of **plot**, this chapter represents a crisis which the rest of the novel will seek to resolve, yet it is oddly anti-climactic. It is only later that we learn of the events in the cave from Adela's point of view, and then sporadically and not very clearly. There is a deliberate **lacuna** in the text at this point which teases and resists the reader's wish to 'know' what happened to Adela in the cave. Of course, by narrating events in this way and withholding information, E.M. Forster maximises the dramatic surprise of Aziz's arrest at the end of the chapter. The incomplete party at the caves with its disruptions and unexpected absences and presences, continues to develop the **theme** of invitations developed in the first section (see Chapters 3, 5, 6, and 7 and Recurring Themes).

**Chin-chin**  jocular imperial toast

chapter 17   **An interview between Fielding and Turton at the railway station**

The Collector, beside himself with rage and emotion, informs Fielding that Aziz has 'insulted' Adela. Fielding cannot believe it and his rationality angers Turton still more. He blames newcomers with their modern ideas for putting aside the simple rule that different races should never be intimate socially. He invites Fielding to a meeting at the club and, stopping some looting of Aziz's possessions, leaves the station full of racial hatred.

> This chapter illustrates E.M. Forster's belief in the power of rationality and personal relationships. Also it shows his mistrust of 'herd' instinct (p. 159). Fielding refuses to be drawn into a prefabricated mass hysteria around the issues of race and group loyalty without seeking to find out the facts. Turton, standing in the station waiting-room 'like a god in a shrine' (p.157), confirms Mrs Moore's assertion to Ronny that in India 'Englishmen like posing as gods' (Chapter 5, p. 63). His orders as he leaves the station show the command of the British imperialist in action, despite his personal feelings.

> **chuprassy**　minor official attendant

## CHAPTER 18　Fielding talks to McBryde at the police-station

There is a short description of McBryde, the District Superintendent of Police, and his criminal racial theories. He informs Fielding of the changes and cites the broken field-glasses as evidence. Fielding asks to see Adela who is ill in hospital in the hope of averting charges but he is denied. He is also refused permission to see Aziz.

> It is evident that Aziz has already been judged guilty before he has even been charged. McBryde is not seen as a sinister or even unsympathetic character but his racial 'theories' predispose him to view all Indians as potential criminals, a view reinforced by folk memories of the 'Mutiny' of 1857–8. All so-called 'evidence' like Aziz's possession of the broken field-glasses, the contents of his pocket-book and the photograph of his dead wife (see Chapter 6, p. 68), are given the worst possible interpretation. As regards any sexual behaviour, it is clear a double standard operates between Europeans and Indians. Indians are 'pitch' (p. 163) and to touch pitch is to be defiled. McBryde appeals to Fielding's race loyalty as an Englishman, not to his sense of justice as an individual.

> ***Bhagavad Gita***　sacred book of Hinduism

CHAPTER 19  Fielding talks to Hamidullah. A conversation between
            Fielding and Professor Godbole about events in the
            caves and the nature of good and evil

Despite his disappointment with Hamidullah's caution, Fielding
commits himself to Aziz's cause. However, he learns that an eminent
anti-British lawyer from Calcutta is being brought into the case and
regrets having to take sides. He sees difficulties for himself and 'muddle'
(p. 167) ahead. He goes to the College and tries to clear up the mystery
of a Russell's Viper found in one of the classrooms. Godbole is leaving to
start up a High School in his birthplace at Mau in Central India and
chooses this occasion to ask Fielding's advice about a name for the school.
Fielding is bewildered that Godbole should be concerned with this
matter at such a time. He wants to know Godbole's opinion on Aziz's
guilt or innocence. The professor is charmingly evasive and frustratingly
inconclusive on this issue. Good and evil are performed by the whole
universe not any one individual. They are also both aspects of 'my Lord.'
'He is present in the one, absent in the other' (p. 169). He concludes the
meeting with the story of the Tank of the Dagger in the Marabar Hills.
Fielding visits Aziz in prison who is incoherent with misery and writes a
letter to Adela with no certainty that she will ever be allowed to read it.

> This chapter develops the **theme** of mystery and muddle initiated
> in Chapter 7 (see p. 79). Professor Godbole is not a major character,
> quite insignificant for the workings of the **plot**, yet his interventions
> carry significant weight. This chapter should be compared with his
> song to Krishna in Chapter 7 in the 'Mosque' section and his divine
> dance in the Gokul Ashtami festival in Chapter 33 that introduces
> the 'Temple' section. The matter of the Russell's Viper picks up a
> thread of snake **imagery** and that of other poisonous creatures that
> runs through the text. See Aziz's warning to Mrs Moore in Chapter
> 2 (pp. 39–40), the cobra that may be only a tree-stump (p. 139) and
> the echoes in the caves that are compared to snakes 'writhing' (p.
> 144) in Chapter 14. The snake is a traditional Christian **symbol** of
> evil. Godbole's metaphysical speculations on the matter of guilt and
> innocence, good and evil, are important for the wider concerns of
> the novel. The events in the caves, whatever they were, have
> somehow crystallised the race hatred that always simmers below the

surface of life at Chandrapore. All are implicated in the good and the evil. As regards the fiasco of the caves: Aziz's invitation was not sincerely meant and his hospitality over possessive, Adela was tactless, repressing uncomfortable emotional truths about her relation with Ronny, the guide was remiss in his duties, Fielding and Godbole missed the train. 'When evil occurs, it expresses the whole of the universe' (p. 169). Godbole's concluding anecdote about the Tank of the Dagger seems to suggest a more hopeful message of guilt and redemption.

**Russell's viper**  deadly Indian snake
**pargana**  district

CHAPTER 20    **The gathering at the club and a crisis meeting. Fielding declares his belief in Aziz's innocence and resigns**

Adela's plight has become a focus for Anglo-Indian group solidarity. Feeling threatened, the local Europeans gather together at the club to be reassured by the Collector. News arrives that Adela is out of danger. Major Callendar puts the worst possible construction on the events leading up to Adela's flight from the caves and begins to bate Fielding. When he refuses to stand up on Heaslop's entrance, Fielding is called to account by the Collector and makes his personal statement. He asserts his belief in Aziz's innocence, declaring his intention to leave India if he is proved wrong. He is ejected from the club.

The group hysteria of the English is treated **satirically** in this chapter. Their attitude is shown to be an absurd overreaction to the actual situation. As the reference to Lucknow suggests, they are reliving the tribal myths of the Indian Mutiny in a rather self-indulgent way. Adela is the innocent victim of racial abuse, and Ronny, 'bearing the sahib's cross' (p. 175), is a martyr. Callendar is the worst offender and the most bigoted in his attitude; the drunken subaltern who had unknowingly played polo with Aziz in Chapter 6, is the most comical. This chapter shows Fielding in a good light as he stands up against group pressure and prejudice for the rights of the individual. However, he regrets his rudeness to Ronny

Heaslop and feels an obscure sense of disappointment and inadequacy as he looks at the deceptive twilight beauty of the Marabar Hills.

Although the tableau of Mrs Blakiston and her child (p. 172) **ironically** refers to the terrors of the Indian Mutiny and the popular images that created in the public mind, E.M. Forster is also placing events in Chandrapore in the context of a more recent atrocity. The references to 'special trains', 'flogging natives', 'calling the troops' and 'clearing the bazaars' refer to the popular unrest in the Punjab just before E.M. Forster's second visit to India in 1921 and, in particular, the Amritsar Massacre of 1919 when General Dyer fired on unarmed protesters. In the subsequent disturbances, women and children were evacuated from the area on special trains and a Miss Sherwood was badly beaten. Six Indians thought to be involved were publicly flogged as well as other reprisals (see notes to Chapter 24).

**The Residency at Lucknow** scene of a famous siege during the Indian Mutiny (1857)

**Mohurram** Moslem religious festival

**Pallas Athene** Greek goddess of wisdom and protectress of the state, often depicted in armour carrying a spear and shield

**Gurkhas, Rajputs, Jats, Punjabi, Sikhs, Marathas, Bhils, Afridis and Pathans** these are all references to warlike Indian castes and tribes

**Monsalvat** legendary mountain thought to conceal the Holy Grail

**Valhalla** the place of honour for dead heroes in Norse mythology

CHAPTER 21    Fielding visits his new Indian allies. Professor Godbole leaves for his new job

Fielding rides into town which is busy preparing for the Mohurram festival and sees no sign of civil unrest. Preparations for Aziz's defence also continue and Amritrao, the well-known Calcutta lawyer, has agreed to take the case. Fielding would like to discuss his actions with Godbole but the professor is in bed and soon slips quietly away to his new post.

**tazia** float made of bamboo and paper to carry in a procession

CHAPTER 22   Adela's disturbed and uncertain state of mind. The echo and the release of evil (p. 183). Mrs Moore's hostility and belief that Aziz is innocent. 'She has started the machinery; it will work to its end' (p. 192)

Adela recovers at the McBrydes' before returning to Heaslop's bungalow. She has been badly pricked by cactus spines and is abnormally conscious of her body. Her memories of the assault in the cave are vague and brief and her emotional stability is very fragile. She is told of Fielding's letter which suggests that she has made a mistake and of the impending trial. She learns of the withdrawal of Aziz's bail because of unrest during Mohurram, and of another accident in the Nawab Bahadur's car involving Aziz and the Nawab's grandson, Nureddin. Like Mrs Moore (Chapter 14, p. 144–6), she is also troubled by an echo. After the Marabar expedition, Mrs Moore is much changed and has retreated into cynical, irritated indifference. She will not attend the trial and wishes to go home. When Adela begins to doubt that Aziz was the assailant in the cave, Mrs Moore also asserts his innocence but Ronny insists that the law must now take its course.

The echo that featured prominently in Chapter 14 has become a running **motif** in the text. It was mentioned by McBryde in Chapter 18, and considered by Fielding at the end of Chapter 20 before getting further development here. It has undermined Mrs Moore's hold on life as we have been warned it would (Chapter 14, p. 146) and now is part of Adela's hysteria. In her excitable state of mind, it seems that the echo followed her out of the cave and is flooding the world with evil. The fact that it briefly disappears (p. 189) when she declares Aziz innocent suggests that it may be a symptom of her repression and bad faith. Further evidence for this is that she chooses to be angry at Fielding's treatment of Ronny rather than at the contents of his letter. Adela's panic begins after scratching the inner 'skin' of the caves to make the echo. We have learned earlier from McBryde (Chapter 18, p. 161) that after running down the side of the hill, Adela began to 'fling herself about': her dislike of physical contact and the morbid awareness of her own skin after this self-mutilation with the cactus spines is suggestive of some kind of physical revulsion and sexual repression.

CHAPTER 23    Mrs Moore leaves India in 'the twilight of the double vision' (p. 193)

Lady Mellanby, the wife of an important provincial official, offers Mrs Moore a berth in her reserved cabin aboard a P. and O. liner bound for home. Although she is spared the trial, the marriage and the hot weather, Mrs Moore is not grateful. In her despairing apathy 'the horror of the universe and its smallness are both visible at the same time' (p. 193). She is spiritually 'muddled'. However, as the train passes Asirgarh she becomes aware that she has not seen all of India and its great variety contains much more than the echo of the Marabar Caves.

> This short reflective chapter is a pause in the action and similar to Chapters 1, 4, 10 and 12. The authorial **persona** is prominent as we are encouraged to consider Mrs Moore's spiritual condition. The playful 'dear reader' address (p. 194) is a nineteenth-century device that draws us closer to the writer but also reminds us that we *are* readers and that this is a text to be read. Mrs Moore's despair seems one of total reduction; she has lost the wonder as well as the fear of the 'overarching sky' (Chapter 1, p. 30). The **imagery** of the 'undying worm', 'serpent of eternity' and 'maggots' links with the snake imagery used earlier (see notes to Chapter 19). This chapter concludes by **personifying** some of the voices of 'the hundred India' that contradict the nihilistic echoes of the caves.

> **Asirgarh**  historic hill fortress
>
> **Vindhyas**  mountains in central India
>
> **the bilingual rock of Girnar, the statue of Shri Beloga, the ruins of Mandu and Hampi, temples of Khajuraho, gardens of Shalimar**  various exotic sites on a tourist's itinerary of India

CHAPTER 24    The day of the trial. Adela's retraction: 'I'm afraid I have made a mistake' (p. 210)

The trial takes place during the worst of the summer heat. Still troubled by her echo, Adela drives to the court with the Turtons. Attitudes are hardening. There is evidence of growing anti-British feeling in Chandrapore and the English community surrounding Adela are full of hatred for the Indians. Only Ronny will back the right of his deputy,

Das, to preside over the court proceedings. In the court room, Adela's attention is drawn to the beautiful low caste Indian who pulls the punkah to cool the air. McBryde's case for the prosecution is interrupted by a comic struggle over the seating arrangements and then by demands that Mrs Moore should be allowed to testify for the defence. Mahmoud Ali leaves in protest and there is noisy chanting outside the court. Adela give her evidence and relives the experience of the Marabar expedition. As McBryde takes her through their rehearsed interrogation, Adela suddenly realises that Aziz did not follow her into the cave and abruptly withdraws her accusation. Amid scenes of uproar and confusion, the assembly disperses leaving the punkah-wallah to fan the empty court.

This chapter is the **dénouement** or formal resolution of the **plot** around the mystery of the Marabar Caves. The rest of the 'Caves' section is largely a matter of tidying up events in the aftermath of the trial. While the most of the Anglo-Indian community 'are shown in a poor light, Ronny's defence of Das and Adela's stubborn commitment to the truth reveal some of the better qualities of Western civilized values. However, Adela's praying to Jehovah for a favourable verdict and her repression of her emotional doubts also reveal some of the weaknesses and limitations in Western rationality that the caves have exposed. By leading her back through her experiences again, McBryde seems to have unwittingly unblocked or exorcised Adela's fears in some way and so enabled her to confront some truth about herself. The magnificent, near naked figure of the punkah-wallah acts as a **symbol** for the mysterious **'Otherness'** of India. Presiding over the proceedings with more authority than the magistrate, his mere presence diminishes the trial as petty and insignificant. The chant of 'Esmiss Esmoor' shows that not all echoes are evil. Mrs Moore's return as a beneficent 'Hindu goddess' (p. 207) pervades the court suggesting that her influence helps to turn the trial in Aziz's favour. We learn later (Chapter 26, p. 226) that she is already dead at this point.

Mrs Turton's angry demand that the Indians 'ought to crawl from here to the caves on their hands and knees whenever an Englishwoman's in sight' (p. 200) recalls General Dyer's notorious 'crawling order'. During the Amritsar disturbances of 1919 (see notes to Chapter 20), he ordered all Indians passing through the lane where Miss Sherwood was attacked to crawl on their hands and knees until forced to cancel the order by the Punjab government.

**Balder**  Norse god of light
**Persephone**  Greek goddess associated with the spring
**Lakshmi**  Hindu goddess of wealth
**sweepers**  latrine cleaners
**punkah-wallah**  servant who operates a fan
**Andamans**  the Andaman Islands in the bay of Bengal had a penal colony

CHAPTER 25    **The aftermath of the trial. Fielding rescues Adela. A victory procession. Aziz and Fielding are separated. Dr Panna Lal averts a major disturbance at the Minto Hospital**

Adela is swept away from the English by the crowd and Fielding puts her in his carriage for her own safety. They are pulled in procession through the bazaar by his students and finally left at his residence. Fielding is impatient to be with his friend but feels responsible for her and gives her sanctuary. Meanwhile Aziz is drawn in the procession towards the Minto Hospital to 'rescue' Nureddin. Callendar's intemperate rages have been overheard and the crowd is convinced that Nureddin has been tortured after his car accident (see Chapter 22). A potentially dangerous incident is averted when Panna Lal humiliates himself to appease the protesters and brings Nureddin from the hospital. The Nawab Bahadur embraces his grandson and makes a speech renouncing his title for 'plain Mr Zulfiqar' (p. 216) and the crowd disperses.

This chapter explores the dangerous volatility of the crowd with a mixture of farce and menace. Fielding and Aziz are kept apart by racial loyalty as much as by accident and this anticipates their growing estrangement later.

**sais**  groom
**tatties**  screens made from dried grass
**hakim**  doctor

chapter 26   Conversation between Adela and Fielding at the
             Government College. Arrival of Hamidullah. His
             hostility to Adela. Ronny arrives with the news of his
             mother's death. Fielding allows Adela to stay at the
             college. The question of compensation

Later in the day, Fielding and Adela discuss the events in the cave. Adela
confesses that she has been unwell ever since Fielding's tea-party at the
garden-house. Her 'echo' has finally disappeared, and Fielding suggests
that McBryde had unwittingly 'exorcised' her in some way during the trial
(p. 219) but both admit to the limitations of reason in trying to explain
such mysterious events. Adela may have experienced an hallucination or
it may have been the guide. At this point Hamidullah arrives to take
Fielding away to Aziz's victory celebrations at Dilkusha, the Nawab
Bahadur's country house. He is full of bitterness and very hostile to the
suggestion that Adela might remain under Fielding's protection. Ronny
than arrives searching for Adela and after some awkward negotiations,
it is agreed that Adela can stay at the college. We learn that Mrs
Moore has died and been buried at sea. On their way to Dilkusha,
Fielding is horrified to learn that Amritrao, the Calcutta lawyer, is setting
the sum that Adela should pay Aziz in compensation at twenty thousand
rupees.

> The belief of the Indians that 'The English always stick together'
> (Chapter 25, p. 213) gets some justification here. Fielding cannot
> help but be sympathetic to Adela and Ronny, despite the harm
> done to Aziz. Humidullah's belief that he is 'silly and weak' (p. 226)
> echoes the judgement of the English club. (See Mrs Turton's 'weak,
> weak, weak' in Chapter 24, p. 200.) Personal relationships seem
> vulnerable when caught up in the hostilities of race and politics.
> The chapter ends with Fielding despairing of human nature with
> the **motif** of the Marabar Hills reappearing again (p. 227 which
> refers us back to the end of Chapter 20, pp. 179–80).

> **Dak Bungalow**  official rest-house for travellers
> **band-ghari**  a closed carriage

CHAPTER 27    The question of compensation. Strains in the
              friendship between Aziz and Fielding

After the victory feast, Fielding and Aziz talk under the stars on the roof
of the Nawab Bahadur's house. Aziz is calm and gracious, but bitter. He
will leave Imperial India to work in some Moslem state far away from the
British. Fielding begs him to forgo his compensation as it would ruin
Adela. He will ensure that Aziz receives a full apology. But Aziz feels no
generosity towards the British and finds Fielding too cold and rational.
Only Mrs Moore is 'an Oriental' (p. 231) in spirit, a preference that
Fielding finds difficult to understand as she has done Aziz no concrete
good. Aziz will consult Mrs Moore on the matter of compensation, not
realising that she is already dead.

> This chapter explores the fissures that are beginning to develop
> between the two men, particularly Aziz's lack of Western chivalry
> towards Adela. Fielding is made conscious of his spiritual
> inadequacy as the spirit of Mrs Moore still continues to make its
> presence felt.

**Regulus** Roman general

CHAPTER 28    Two contrasting responses to the death of Mrs
              Moore

Mrs Moore's death casts a shadow over the ship which is cast off when it
reaches Port Said. Back in Chandrapore a cult springs up around the
memory of an English woman who has been killed by her son because she
wished to save an Indian's life. Tombs of 'Esmiss Esmoor' appear. Ronny
is guilty but irritated and unrepentant. He will not marry Adela now and
plans to erect a memorial tablet in his mother's church at home.

> The **omniscient narrator** comments on the contrasting attitudes to
> death and immortality held by Indians and British. While for the
> local Indians the memory of Mrs Moore lives on in a mythologised
> form, Ronny attitude is cold and spiritually arid. His lack of charity
> extends to Adela too. E.M. Forster uses the technique of **free
> indirect style** to mime as well as comment on Ronny's limited
> language and imagination in phrases like 'Presumably she goes to

heaven, anyhow she clears out', and 'She belonged to the callow academic period of his life which he had outgrown – Grasmere, serious talks and walks, that sort of thing' (p. 234).

CHAPTER 29    **Aziz gives up his claim for compensation. Fielding and Adela talk again. 'A friendliness, as of dwarfs shaking hands' (p. 239). Ronny breaks off the engagement and Adela returns to England**

The Lieutenant-Governor of the Province visits Chandrapore and congratulates Fielding for his sensible attitude. Fielding learns to respect Adela as she struggles to accept her limitations with humility and he finds Aziz's attitude rather overbearing. He manages to persuade Aziz to forgo his compensation through the influence of Mrs Moore's memory. When he learns that her engagement is broken off, Fielding visits Adela and they discuss the events in the caves for the last time. They feel drawn together in their inadequacy and inability to explain what has happened. Is life is a mystery or a muddle? 'They had not the apparatus for judging' (p. 239). They feel dwarfed by the immensity of the universe. Scandal pursues Adela to the end of her stay in India as her servant, Anthony, attempts to blackmail her before her departure, but once in the Suez Canal, she takes fresh stock of her situation and resolves to meet Mrs Moore's other children on her return to England.

This chapter is part of the long, drawn-out **closure** of the Marabar Cave episode which has been the novel's substantial **plot**. Many conventional novels would seek to resolve the major issues through a marriage at this point in the text, but it is clear that is not an option here; Adela and Fielding, though now friends, are not seeking love. Much remains tentative and unresolved as Western reason fails to provide an adequate, satisfying answer to the challenge and mystery of the Marabar Caves.

**Lesseps statue** Ferdinand de Lesseps (1805–94) was responsible for the building of the Suez Canal

CHAPTER 30    An attempted Hindu-Moslem entente. Aziz considers
poetry, Indian nationalism and leaving British India.
Rumours concerning Fielding and Adela

In the aftermath of the trial, Hindus and Moslems seek to improve their
relations in Chandrapore. Das visits Aziz at the hospital and asks him to
write a poem for his brother-in-law's magazine. Both are superficially
moved but also realise the depth of their differences. Aziz finds it
impossible to write a poem for a modern nationalist readership. He does
not wish to engage in politics like his friend Hamidullah and declares a
wish to work in a Hindu state. He learns that rumours are spreading
concerning the relationship between Adela and Fielding. As they go to
see Aziz's children behind the purdah, Hamidullah complains of the
reluctance of Indian women to modernise.

A chapter that focuses on the Indian community and the political
aspects of the story (compare Chapters 2, 6 and 9). It is clear that
anti-British sentiment will not be sufficient to unite the various
political and ethnic factions in India. Although hardened by his
experience and seeking to become an Pan-Indian nationalist, Aziz
remains a romantic in matters of art and still wishes to write about
'the decay of Islam and the brevity of love' (p. 242).

There was a brief attempt to secure an Hindu-Moslem alliance
between the Indian National Congress and the Khalifat movement
during the period of E.M. Forster's second stay in India.

**bulbuls** nightingales
**the Politicals** Political Agents, the British advisers in Native States
**Elephants' Ears** Indian coconut sweet
**begum** Moslem lady of rank

CHAPTER 31    The final estrangement between Aziz and Fielding:
'the unexplained residue of the Marabar contributing'
(p. 252). Fielding to return to England on leave

Racial division, suspicion and resentment over Adela cause a rapid
cooling of the intimacy between Aziz and Fielding. Fielding is shocked
by the suggestion of an affair with Adela and, although Aziz is full
of remorse, barriers of language and culture prove impossible to surmount

on either side. Aziz is not avaricious but cannot rid himself of the thought that he has been tricked out of his rightful compensation, nor the suspicion that Fielding returns to England to marry Adela. Fielding visits the Club to find that everything and nothing has changed there. McBryde's adultery with Miss Derek has been discovered, further exposing the double standards of the British in sexual matters (see Chapter 18, pp. 162–4). Aziz makes his excuses and is away with his children in Mussoorie when Fielding leaves for England.

> After the break-up of the engagement between Adela and Ronny, the apparent failure of Fielding's friendship with Aziz concludes this section of the book on a saddened, muted note. The echoes of the Marabar Caves (p. 248) still reverberate and seem destined to frustrate all efforts to bridge the gap between people, races and cultures.

> **almeira** cupboard, wardrobe
> **durry** carpet

CHAPTER 32    **Fielding's passage from India**

Fielding returns to the familiarity of the Mediterranean with relief and relishes the harmony between landscape and architecture in Venice with a new-found pleasure. The European summer brings hope and a sense of renewal.

> Rather like Chapter 23 describing Mrs Moore's departure from Bombay, and Adela's new resolve as she passes through the Suez Canal at the end of Chapter 29 (p. 240), this brief **coda** to the second section offers Fielding a different perspective on life from that dominated by the 'extraordinary' Marabar Caves.

PART 3: TEMPLE

CHAPTER 33    **The birth of Krishna festival at Mau. 'God si Love'**
                         **(p. 258). Professor Godbole's dance. Mrs Moore, the**
                         **wasp and the stone**

After a break of two years, the narrative resumes in the Hindu state of Mau at the height of the Gokul Ashtami festival in the wet monsoon season. As Minister of Education, Professor Godbole leads his choir in song and dance as the celebrations move towards their climax in the birth of Krishna. All seems chaotic confusion and muddle. An English waltz competes with Hindu chanting and an inscription has been pinned on the wall that reads 'God si Love'. In a trance-like state, Godbole seeks to imitate God and embrace the infinite; the memory of Mrs Moore and the image of a wasp on a stone come unsolicited into his mind. He can love the woman and the wasp equally, but not the stone. The aged Rajah joins the celebrations and, on the stroke of midnight, amid much noisy celebration, Krishna is born. Much play and practical jokes follow as the sick Rajah is taken back to the care of his physician, Dr Aziz.

This last introductory chapter (see Chapters 1 and 12) sets the tone of the 'Temple' section. As the 'Mosque' section focused on hope and aspiration in the Indian spring, and the 'Caves' section on disillusion and racial division in the Indian summer, so the dominant mood of this final section is reconciliation and forgiveness at the height of the rainy season. Once again, the narrator assumes the **persona** of a rather bemused European describing a Hindu religious festival without much comprehension. To Western eyes, all seems 'a frustration of reason and form' and the final message of India may be the comical 'God si Love' (p. 258). Godbole's mystic dance epitomises the mysterious muddle that is India and his call to God, 'Come, come, come, come' (p. 263), echoes his song at the end of Chapter 7 (p. 87). His trance-like connection of Mrs Moore and the wasp also refers us back to the end of Chapter 3 ('pretty dear', p. 50) where Mrs Moore shows Christian charity to the sleeping insect. So here, briefly, Brahmin and Christian become one with the wasp in love, but Godbole's failure to imitate God and love the stone equally seems an oblique reference to the intransigent Marabar Caves and return him to the limitations of time and space. When midnight strikes, all Western rational categories ('foreigners, birds, caves, railways, and the stars', p. 260) collapse into a celebration of divine love. In the farcical antics that follow, mystery and muddle become the same thing. The rather impressionistic, densely poetic allusiveness of this opening chapter signal a rather different world from the harsh, cause-and-effect logic of the 'Caves' section where the 'machinery' of British justice 'will work to its end' (Chapter 22, p. 192).

The Hindu state of Mau that features in this section is based on two Indian native states, Chhatarpur and Dewas, that E.M. Forster visited in 1912. Subsequently he was private secretary to the Maharajah of Dewas Senior on his second visit to India in 1921. The festival of Gokul Ashtami described in the 'Temple' section is based on his own experiences at this time which may be read in his travel book, *The Hill of Devi* (1953).

**Tukaram**  a Mahratta saint
**Kansa**  Indian king of Muthura who sought to kill the baby Krishna
**'Nights of Gladness'**  a waltz composed in 1912 by Charles Ancliffe (1880–1952)
**Gokul**  the legendary birthplace of Krishna
**the wanton dairymaids of Brindaban**  Krishna played with them in his youth
**Pandava wars**  the subject of the Indian epic, the *Mahabharata*

CHAPTER 34   **Aziz has settled at Mau with his children. The break with Fielding over his marriage. Fielding arrives on an official visit with his wife and her brother**

Through Godbole's influence, Aziz is now the court physician at Mau. He hates the English and refuses to answer Fielding's letters because he believes he has married Adela Quested. Although he seeks to modernise his poetry, Aziz still writes of the pathos of defeated Islam, and lives comfortably enough under the watchful eye of the Political Agent of the British. When he learns from Godbole of Fielding's arrival on an official visit as an Education Inspector, Aziz is determined to avoid him if he can.

After the religious enthusiasm of Chapter 33, this chapter moves us back into the plot and the broken friendship of Aziz and Fielding. We learn that even though 'The fissures of the Indian soil are infinite' (p. 264), the Moslem Aziz is more accepted by the tolerant Hindus than by the representative of the British Raj who still seeks to make life difficult for him.

**Brahman** Hindu priestly caste
**Plassy** The Battle of Plassey (1757) where Robert Clive defeated the
Indians and seized Bengal
**bhakti** religious devotion

CHAPTER 35   **The story of the Shrine of the Head and the Body.**
**Aziz meets Fielding and his brother-in-law at the old**
**fort. Bee stings at the Shrine of the Head. Aziz learns**
**of his mistake but refuses to be reconciled**

Long before Aziz, a young Moslem had come to Mau. He obeyed an
order from his mother to 'free prisoners' but had been executed by the
police. His head and his body had fallen at different places where shrines
had been built to honour him. He is now regarded as a local saint. Aziz
and his children walk to the Shrine of the Head where prisoners from the
jail are exercising. One of their number will be freed as part of the climax
of the Gokul Ashtami festival. Fielding and Ralph Moore arrive and
Ralph is stung by bees in the shrine. Aziz is cold and hostile, refusing to
cooperate with the visitors' desire to see the torchlight procession to the
great tank which will conclude the religious ceremonies. He discovers
that Fielding has married Stella Moore, Mrs Moore's daughter by her
second marriage, not Adela Quested. He has not read Fielding's letters
and has been deceived by Mahmoud Ali but it changes nothing.
However, returning home he is oddly elated by the memory of Mrs
Moore.

The fable of the young Moslem saint, the two shrines and the toy
mosque, illustrate the inclusive, all-embracing nature of Hindu
worship. The split between head and body also suggest the divisions
existing in the human condition that all religions seek to mend. At
this point, Aziz and Fielding cannot come together but the memory
of 'Esmiss Esmoor ...' (p. 272; see also Chapter 24, p. 207) seems
to promise her healing influence is at work. The intrigue involving
the concealment of the old Rajah's death makes the more mundane
point that politics and human calculations continue despite
religious yearning and aspiration.

**Durbar** the court of a Native State

CHAPTER 36    **Aziz visits the State Guest House. 'Then you are an Oriental ... Mosque, caves, mosque, caves. And here he was starting again' (p. 280). God is 'thrown away' (p. 282): the final ceremony on the lake and the collision of the boats**

As preparations continue for the final procession to the great Mau tank, Aziz rides over to the Guest House with ointment for Ralph Moore's stings. On the way, he sees the English party set out by boat to view the climax of the festivities on the shore. He enters the Guest House boldly (compare his timid approach to Major Callendar's bungalow in Chapter 2) believing it to be deserted and impudently reads private letters from Adela Quested and Ronny Heaslop. He is disturbed by Ralph Moore who has stayed behind because of his bee stings. Aziz treats Ralph cruelly at first but, as the noise from the procession increases at the release of the prisoner, he finds himself softening to Mrs Moore's son. He invites Ralph out on the water to see the festival's end. The palanquin of Krishna appears with its singing votaries. As the rainstorm increases a servitor carries the clay model of Gokul village and its effigies into the water to melt away. Simultaneously, the two boats collide tipping their occupants into the water amid great confusion and noise. 'That was the climax, as far as India admits of one' (p. 283).

> Aziz's bitterness finally yields to the influence of religious rejoicing and the benign spirit of Mrs Moore which seems to live on in her son. Aziz's impulsive tribute, 'Then you are an Oriental', echoes his earlier words to Mrs Moore in the mosque at Chandrapore (Chapter 2, p. 41). So one cycle is completed and another begins. His invitation to take Ralph out on the water is the last, and most successful, of the many invitations in the novel because it is intimate and spontaneous. Aziz's reading of the letters shows the English gradually reasserting their social bonds after the events at the Marabar Caves, but this is superficial compared to the divine confusion and re-unification that takes place in the tank. Here all is mystery and muddle as the religious offerings of Gokul Ashtami, the stolen letters, Aziz, Fielding, Ralph and Stella, all come together in a wet

confusion. The dominance of water **imagery** here, as in this section throughout, suggests liberation, spiritual healing and reconciliation.

The details of the final procession to the tank are drawn from E.M. Forster's own observations of the Gokul Ashtami festival at Dewas Senior which may be read in *The Hill of Devi* (1953).

**Indra** the supreme deity in Hindu mythology

**Sweepers' Band** Sweepers belonged to 'the untouchables', the lowest caste in Hindu society

**palanquin** covered litter borne on poles

**chhatri** shrine

**Radhakrishna Krishnaradha** Radha is Krishna's consort. The two names are sung together and in reverse

**Ganpati** Hindu god with an elephant's head

CHAPTER 37   The final ride of Aziz and Fielding. 'Why can't we be friends now?' … 'No, not yet' … 'No, not there' (p. 289)

Fielding's official visit has not been a success. Godbole has been avoiding him as the King-Emperor George Fifth High School has been converted into a granary and Fielding cannot view the matter as lightly as he might once have done. He and Aziz have recovered their former ease together but they know that they will never meet again. After the events in the tank, Aziz is now reconciled to Adela and Fielding seeks his advice over Stella. Fielding's marriage has had its difficulties; Stella is searching for some meaning in life that Fielding finds inexplicable and closed to him, but the experiences at Mau are already having a beneficial effect on their relationship. As they ride through the jungle enjoying a political debate, Fielding mocks Aziz's dreams of Indian nationhood and Aziz tells Fielding that they will only remain friends when the English are thrown out of India. The two men come together in one final gesture of emotional intimacy, but the Indian earth and sky intervene to forbid their friendship.

The earth and sky have dominated and frustrated human endeavour from the opening chapter. Some of the beguiling 'hundred voices of

India' have given hope but others, like the Marabar echoes, have been less accommodating. Although the novel ends on a note of muted hope – 'not yet' implies maybe sometime and 'not there' implies maybe somewhere else – it is clear that perfect harmony between individuals as well as races remains an aspiration rather than a real possibility. The tension between optimism and pessimism that have been a feature of the novel remain intact to the very end.

# CRITICAL APPROACHES

## FLAT AND ROUND CHARACTERS

In his critical work, *Aspects of the Novel* (1927), E.M. Forster made an interesting distinction between characters in novels that are 'flat' and those that are 'round'. Flat characters are 'constructed around a single idea or quality', easily recognised and remembered, and best 'when they are comic'. Round characters are capable of surprising us 'in a convincing way' and only they are able to 'perform tragically' or touch our sympathies more subtly. As a basis for discussion, this distinction is useful but any attentive reading of *A Passage to India* will reveal that most characters have a capacity for sudden insight, sympathy and development. Apparently 'flat', minor characters like the garrulous Miss Derek or Hamidullah's lazy dependent, Mohammed Latif, have the quality that E.M. Forster praised in Jane Austen: 'They function all round, and even if her plot made greater demands on them than it does, they would still be adequate'.

However, it is fair to say that, broadly, 'flatness' is reserved for ethnic groups, social **satire**, and **comedy of manners**, 'roundness' for moral development and the genuinely complex exploration of relationships. E.M. Forster's comic abilities are shown to best advantage in the set-pieces involving the Anglo-Indians like the Bridge Party (Chapter 5), the scenes at the Club (Chapters 3, 20) and the trial (Chapter 24). He is less secure with the indigenous Indians because he knows less, and successful 'flat' characterisation requires an intimate understanding of class and social type from inside a culture and for readers of that culture. He does attempt to explore the rivalries between Hindu and Moslem in, say, the grouping around Aziz's sickbed in Chapter 9 but he cannot quite eradicate an innately superior **eurocentric** point of view that patronises and so softens the **satirical** effect. Ronny Heaslop is a triumph of characterisation. We recognise E.M. Forster's scorn because Ronny actually wants to become a flat Anglo-Indian stereotype and mouth their clichés, and yet we also respond to those more complicated scenes with Adela and his mother (see Chapters 3, 5 and 8) which bring out a latent complexity, his potential for 'roundness'.

## ADELA QUESTED AND CYRIL FIELDING

Thoughtful, brave, caring and decent, Adela and Fielding would be the obvious candidates for **heroine** and **hero** in earlier E.M. Forster novels; they so obviously carry his own tolerant, liberal values. Yet our final image of them together is of 'dwarfs shaking hands' (Chapter 29, p. 239). For Adela in the most dramatic way possible, for Fielding in a more oblique manner (see Chapter 20, pp. 179–80, Chapter 26, p. 227) they are tested and falter before the challenge of the Marabar Hills. The best of civilised Western values and the qualities of Western rationalism are inadequate when confronted by vastness and confusion of India. Initially Fielding is hostile to Adela, considering her a 'prig' (Chapter 11, p. 120), but Adela's courageous honesty at the trial brings them closer together in mutual respect. Yet they do not become the lovers of a more conventional fiction, and their new-found friendship does not force a heterosexual marriage **closure** on the novel. They leave India separately, each registering relief on their return to a more 'normal' European scene.

## DR AZIZ

E.M. Forster is rather proprietorial in his treatment of Aziz, and Adela's private thoughts on entering the cave, 'What a handsome little Oriental he was' (Chapter 15, p. 148), seems to reflect his own attitude. Aziz is characterised as attractive but unreliable. He is treated affectionately and sympathetically, but also patronised as excitable, over-demonstrative, easily jealous. Although he is seen to dwell too much on an idealised Islamic past, his quest for the perfect 'Friend who never comes yet is not entirely disproved' (Chapter 9, p. 108) seems to express something of E.M. Forster's own erotic yearnings. As regards the **plot**, E.M. Forster has little interest in him after his arrest until the final extended **coda** of reconciliation in the third section. He is absent from the build-up and drama of the trial where the focus shifts to Adela. E.M. Forster uses him as a scapegoat and as a focus for the hostility between the two communities but the absence of any prison scenes in the novel ensures that the political and racial aspects of the story are not allowed to draw our attention away from the personal drama.

## Mrs MOORE AND PROFESSOR GODBOLE

Both these characters are not essential to the plot yet are clearly very significant. To a degree, they have a **symbolic** function; they carry and articulate many of the **themes** in the novel. They do not have a consistent presence. Mrs Moore is summarily dismissed before the trial to return in spirit as the Hindu goddess 'Esmiss Esmoor' (Chapter 24, p. 207). Godbole, too, has brief but significant appearances. He is always disappearing at critical times but his discussion of good and evil (Chapter 19, pp. 168–9) is seminal and puts the events in the Marabar Caves in their context. His divine trance that introduces the final section (Chapter 33), expresses E.M. Forster's desire for an all-encompassing acceptance and charity. Both demonstrate the best spirituality that their respective cultures can aspire to. Mrs Moore's 'poor little talkative Christianity' (Chapter 14, p. 146) is seen as ultimately vulnerable to the negative echo of the Marabar Caves, but her spirit and body (through her son Ralph) live on as a healing presence in the third section of the novel. Godbole's Hinduism is more robust and can accept both muddle and mystery (see Recurring Themes).

## RECURRING THEMES

## THE TITLE

'Passage' is a word of layered meaning in this text. There is, of course, the physical passage of Europeans to India, the move from the familiar into the unknown. As in 'rites of passage', the word suggests a move from a simple to a more complex mode of existence. The word also alerts us to the 'quest' theme in the novel. Adela wants to see 'the *real* India' (Chapter 3, p. 42) and one **plot** strand is the disastrous expedition to the Marabar Caves, a journey that destroys illusions and crushes human aspirations. 'Passage' also has the metaphysical connotations of a more spiritual journey. E.M. Forster once wrote that the theme of the novel was 'the search of the human race for a more lasting home' and the novel's title refers to Walt Whitman's 'Passage to India' (1871), a nineteenth-century poem celebrating the opening of the Suez Canal. Whitman uses the occasion to urge a new synthesis between Western technology and Eastern spiritualism, a 'Passage to more than India', in a mood of exultant optimism:

> Sail forth – steer for the deep water only,
> Reckless O soul, exploring, I with thee, and thou with me,
> For we are bound where mariner has not yet dared to go,
> And we will risk the ship, ourselves and all.

E.M. Forster's sceptical twentieth-century novel casts doubt on Whitman's wild romanticism, yet still urges spiritual aspiration, the need for a quest to find some harmony between the human race and the universe in which we find ourselves: 'a passage not easy, not now, not here, not to be apprehended except when it is unattainable' (Chapter 36, p. 283).

## 'ONLY CONNECT ...'

The phrase 'only connect' is from *Howards End* (1910), one of E.M. Forster's earlier novels, but it is a relevant thematic concern in all his work, and no more so than in *A Passage to India*. E.M. Forster was a liberal who sought to reconcile conflicting forces in all aspects of human life. This effort is tested to the utmost in the harsh, complex world of this novel where 'the spirit of the Indian earth ... tries to keep men in compartments' (Chapter 13, p. 129). Broadly, E.M. Forster's attempts at 'connection' may be categorised as personal, racial and religious, although, of course, these categories overlap. The novel opens with a dialogue between two Indians debating 'whether or no it is possible to be friends with an Englishman' (Chapter 2, p. 31) and the main focus of the book is the growing friendship between Aziz and Fielding across the racial divide, the brutal crisis of the Marabar disaster, and the gradual estrangement between them that follows. The most successful connections between individuals, it seems, are unpremeditated moments of grace, or luck, that are not sustainable through normal social life. An example of the first is the moment of magical intimacy between Aziz and Mrs Moore at the mosque (Chapter 2), and, of the second, Aziz's polo practice with the subaltern on the Maidan (Chapter 6).

Attempts at connection between racial groups illustrate the divisive aspects of colonial occupation in the cultural and religious melting-pot that is India. The power of the Raj rests, it seems, on suspicion and hostility: 'One touch of regret ... would have made him [Ronny] a different man, and the British Empire a different institution' (Chapter 5, p. 64). It is in vain that Mrs Moore calls for 'Goodwill and more goodwill and more goodwill' (Chapter 5, p. 64), and Aziz for 'Kindness, more kindness, and even after that more kindness' (Chapter 11, p. 118). At the so-called Bridge Party (Chapter 5) the rulers and ruled look at each other across the tennis lawns as if across an immense chasm. When the English arrivals try to establish some rapport with Mrs Bhattacharya and her friends, confusion and misunderstanding inevitably follow. Tensions and mistrust also exist between the Indians themselves. Quarrels break out around Aziz's sickbed (Chapter 9) and the hapless Dr Panna Lal plays the fool in order to pacify an ugly mob outside the hospital (Chapter 25). Even after the trial when Aziz is a nationalist hero, he and Das can sense the mutual mistrust in each other's hearts: 'Life is not easy as we know it on the earth' (Chapter 30, p. 242).

From the opening chapter, this human drama is played out against the elemental opposition of the earth and the 'overarching sky' (p. 30) as E.M. Forster seeks to find some hope for a satisfying relationship between the human race, the material world and the universe beyond. This threatening, wider context for human endeavour is one that the Anglo-Indians seek to ignore in their insulated club activities but Mrs Moore can feel 'A sudden sense of unity, of kinship with the heavenly bodies' (Chapter 3, p. 46) and is moved to loving sympathy with the Indian wasp who knows no distinction between indoors and outside. Such moments of reaching-out beyond the self are brief like the 'Little ineffectual unquenchable flames' of Aziz's well-wishers (Chapter 9, p. 109) but they represent an enduring need. For a while it seems that the Indian earth will thwart all such aspirations and it moves to interdict the continued companionship of Aziz and Fielding in the final paragraph of the novel. However, part of E.M. Forster's achievement is to make the reader feel that this is not the final word, 'the unattainable Friend' remains a friend still and the 'eternal promise' that 'haunts our consciousness' (Chapter 10, p. 115–16) is never entirely withdrawn.

## COMMANDS AND INVITATIONS

The first part of the novel is dominated by commands and invitations. In Chapter 2, Aziz's pleasant social evening is interrupted by a command from his senior, Major Callendar, a summons to the Civil Station that leads to humiliation at the hands of Mrs Callendar and Mrs Lesley, but also the unexpected, momentous meeting with Mrs Moore. The English, it seems, are used to command; Ronny calls 'firmly to the moon' (p. 46) in Chapter 3, and the invitation to the Bridge Party has the authority of a command. Unsurprisingly the privileged Indian community is flattered to be invited to the exclusive English Club, but suspicious too. 'You will make yourself chip' Mr Chand warns the Nawab Bahadur (Chapter 4, p. 51). The need to belong to what threatens to be an alien universe is endemic to the human condition and this vulnerability is heightened and emphasised by the British occupation of India. All invitations imply exclusions as we learn in Chapter 4. No earthly invitations can embrace the whole of India so 'All invitations must proceed from heaven perhaps' (p. 52). The Indian countryside calls 'Come, come' through her 'hundred mouths', but 'There was not enough god to go round' (Chapter 8, p. 93).

The theme of invitations gets a particular emphasis in the important Chapter 7. After the failure of the Bridge Party, Fielding's more intimate tea-party is full of promise. The sympathetic accord between him and Aziz is immediate, and Aziz is allowed to demonstrate his frustrated Moslem pride and generosity. But there are ominous developments too. Aziz makes his fateful invitation to the Marabar Caves which will have such catastrophic consequences, Ronny breaks up the party with his insensitive arrogance and Godbole's song, his divine invitation to Krishna, is unsuccessful: 'He neglects to come' (p. 87). Certainly the empty, menacing echo of the Marabar Caves is apparently impervious to all invitations and the middle section of the novel is marked by hostility and division. Before the trial, Adela implores her vengeful Jehovah 'for a favourable verdict' (Chapters 24, p. 196). But even here, the narrative is not without hope. In Chapter 19, the enigmatic, wise

Godbole tells the mystified Fielding that 'absence implies presence', so we are entitled to repeat 'Come, come, come, come' (p. 169).

In the final section, invitations do seem to be briefly answered during the festival of Gokul Ashtami for Krishna is born amid 'universal warmth' (Chapter 33, p. 259). Godbole successfully 'invites' the unsolicited images of Mrs Moore and the wasp in his mystic trance, but his failure with the stone indicates that all human aspiration is limited. Still, Aziz is able to rediscover his generous spirit through the agency of Mrs Moore working through her son. His final invitation to Ralph to row out on the lake does enable a partial reconciliation with Fielding. So although the novel ends on a note of frustration as the two men part, E.M. Forster has shown that the need to invite rather than command is an essential demonstration of our humanity.

## MUDDLE AND MYSTERY

Is India a muddle or a mystery? This theme is initiated in Chapter 7 when Mrs Moore and Adela express their concern over the Bhattacharya fiasco. Mrs Moore likes mysteries but rather dislikes muddles while, for the rational Fielding, 'A mystery is only a rather high-sounding term for a muddle' (p. 79). The capacity for India to create muddle seems limitless. Adela becomes emotionally confused and muddled, Aziz's expedition to the Marabar Caves is beset by muddle, and muddle at the Kawa Dol leads to wholesale social confusion in Chandrapore. In such an atmosphere reason seems powerless to intervene. In vain does Fielding seek some kind of explanation for the events at the caves from Godbole. All the enigmatic professor is prepared to do is make a mystery out of an apparent muddle: 'When evil occurs, it expresses the whole of the universe. Similarly when good occurs ... They are not what we think them, they are what they are, and each of us has contributed to both' (Chapter 19, p. 169). Europeans, it seems, cannot impose any kind of spiritual control over the landscape of India, or draw any consolation from it. In the aftermath of the cave expedition, 'the twilight of the double vision' leads Mrs Moore's into 'spiritual muddledom' (Chapter 23, p. 193), and both Adela and Fielding can only find their bearings once they are safely back in the Mediterranean. In Venice 'a harmony between the works of man and the earth that upholds them' ensures a 'civilization that has escaped muddle' (Chapter 32, p. 253). At their final meeting in India they can only admit that 'perhaps life is a mystery, not a muddle; they could not tell … They had not the apparatus for judging' (Chapter 29, pp. 238–9). The 'Caves' section ends with the parting of Aziz and Fielding amid recrimination and muddle.

However, the muddle of the Marabar Hills is not allowed to have the last word. Even as Mrs Moore departs before the trial some of the voices of 'a hundred Indias' suggests further possibilities and mysteries: "'So you thought an echo was India; you took the Marabar Caves as final?" they laughed. "What have we in common with them, or they with Asirgarh? Goodbye!"' (Chapter 23, p. 195). At Mau, in the celebrations of Gokul Ashtami, muddle becomes mystery and mystery becomes muddle. In the 'frustration of reason and form' that the Western mind terms muddle, 'God si Love', and this may be 'the final message of India' (Chapter 33, p. 258). The echo of the Marabar Caves gave the message that 'Everything exists, nothing has value' (Chapter 14, p. 146), but the birth of Krishna suggests that everything exists and everything has value. In the divine muddle that concludes the festival, boats capsize and confusion heals.

# NARRATIVE TECHNIQUES AND STRUCTURE

## THE THREE SECTIONS

The titles of the three sections underline the significance of religion in the novel. The attempt by men to relate to each other and to the universe in which they find themselves is an important **theme**. The novel's division into 'Mosque', 'Caves' and 'Temple' may be seen to correspond to three great religions present in India, namely Islam, Christianity and Hinduism. In this analysis, the second section is the most problematic. In 'Caves', the British wrathful Jehovah predominates, as does the sterile rationalism of the Imperialist's faith, but the Caves themselves defy representation. Buddhists may claim them, they may be Jain; the suggestion is that they existed long before any human attempt to impose meaning on the universe and their primordial echo seems to undermine the pretensions of all religion.

'Mosque' refers to the mosque where Aziz meets Mrs Moore, and also the garden-house where Fielding holds his tea-party in Chapter 7. The arches of Islam seem to recapitulate the 'overarching sky' of the opening chapter. The architecture of 'Question and Answer' (Chapter 7, p. 79) provides the space for religious aspiration and human intimacy. 'Friend', we are told later (Chapter 31, p. 249), is 'a Persian expression for God' and this section is full of hope, and the appeal to the 'unattainable Friend' (Chapter 10, p. 115) to 'Come, come, come'. Events take place in the Indian spring and there is a predominance of night-scenes under the Indian moon. The stress is on poetry, emotion and feminine intuition. Mrs Moore's friendship with Aziz survives the hostility of Ronny and the cynicism of the Anglo-Indian Club. Adela and Ronny are drawn together by the mystery of the car accident and the friendship of Aziz and Fielding is bonded by the photograph of Aziz's dead wife. Christianity, in the person of the kindly Mrs Moore, is seen at its best. Unlike the old Mr Graysford and the young Mr Sorley (see Chapter 4), she can accept the wasp as 'pretty dear' (Chapter 3, p. 50).

'India does wonders for the judgement, especially during the Hot Weather' (Chapter 3, p. 45). Mr Turton's remark ironically anticipates the disasters of the 'Caves' section. Sun and stone dominate and far from 'doing wonders', the summer heat exposes the fallibility and limitations of Western reason and blights the promise of human relationships. The Indian earth 'tries to keep men in compartments' (Chapter 13, p. 129) and is triumphant in this section. For Fielding, in a moment of depression, 'the fists and fingers of the Marabar' seem to swell 'until they include the whole night sky' (Chapter 26, p. 227). All events in this section lead up to the encounter in the Caves and, in the aftermath, the evil consequences that flow from their undermining echo. The promise of the 'Mosque' section is dissipated and destroyed.

In an interview in 1952 E.M. Forster spoke of the final section of this novel as 'architecturally necessary. I needed a lump, or a Hindu temple if you like – a mountain standing up. It is well placed; and it gathers up some strings'. This section is dominated by the monsoon. The air is 'thick with religion and rain' (Chapter 35, p. 269). 'It gathers up some strings' by recapitulating themes and imagery from the earlier sections in a more positive context once again. The tone is of benign inclusiveness: 'Completeness not reconstruction' (Chapter 33, p. 259).

Hinduism, it seems, is the religion most attune to the challenges and complexities of India. The earth and sky, apart in earlier sections, here lean towards one another, 'about to clash in ecstasy' (Chapter 36, p. 276). A sense of freedom and release is dominant. A prisoner is released from the jail and Aziz is also freed from his cycle of resentment over the Marabar Cave incident (Chapter 36, pp. 279–80). God responds finally to the call 'Come, come, come, come', but is not possessed selfishly, but almost casually 'thrown away' again (Chapter 36, pp. 282–3) as a Moslem, three Europeans and some Hindu religious emblems fall into the water together.

## THREE PLOTS

The action of the novel revolves around three sets of personal relationships. The first is the heterosexual love romance between Adela Quested and Ronny Heaslop; after all, it is this that has brought Mrs Moore and Adela to Chandrapore in the first place. The complications and difficulties of courtship were the mainstay of many fictions in the eighteenth and nineteenth centuries as they are now. Many novelists use the device of marriage to bring a narrative **closure** to their fiction. For the reader, it is a common and generally pleasurable expectation. E.M. Forster also uses the courtship **plot**, but rather perfunctorily. It excites some narrative interest in the early part of the novel. Will Adela marry Ronny? If not, maybe someone else. Fielding perhaps? But after the expedition to the Marabar Caves, such interests fade. E.M. Forster's treatment of heterosexual romance seems to be reflected in Mrs Moore's exasperated irritation: 'Why all this marriage, marriage? … the human race would have become a single person centuries ago if marriage were any use. And all this rubbish about love, love in a church, love in a cave, as if there is the least difference …' (Chapter 22, pp. 188–9).

The developing male friendship between Aziz and Fielding is an important, perhaps *the* most important, plot strand, for the novel ends with their final parting. Because E.M. Forster was homosexual in sexual orientation, the relationship between Aziz and Fielding may be seen as a covert love affair that acts as a foil and rival to the growing friendship between Fielding and Adela. Certainly Fielding's protective defence of Adela ensures Aziz's jealousy and is the main reason why the relationship between the two men falters and loses its impetus after the trial. As homosexuality was potentially a criminal offence for most of E.M. Forster's long life, this aspect of Aziz's role is necessarily coded; his gift of a collar stud (Chapter 7), for example, seems innocent enough but can be read as an erotic **metaphor** for same-sex intimacy and exchange. Given the official public hostility towards homosexuality, it can be seen as inevitable that E.M. Forster could not envisage a continuing intimacy between the two men at the end of the novel.

Finally, there is 'the secret understanding of the heart' (Chapter 2, p. 38) between Aziz and Mrs Moore. This might seem a rather too tenuous and brief a relationship to signify as a plot strand, but, examined in terms of its consequences, the meeting in the mosque between a young Moslem man and an old English lady is momentous indeed. It leads to a further meeting at Fielding's tea-party, the invitation to the Marabar Caves and all that follows from that. Aziz and Mrs Moore never meet again after the Cave expedition but her spirit continues to influence events in oblique, intangible ways. She seems to act as a benign presence during the trial, to prompt Aziz to forgo his claim for compensation, and, finally, to heal the rift between Aziz and Fielding through her son Ralph. This unlikely relationship, then, expresses most poignantly E.M. Forster's belief in the power and significance of disinterested friendship.

## CLOSED AND OPEN FORM

**Plot** is usually seen as a pattern of causality that works through time in a linear sequence. As such, it is driven by the actions of characters as they interact and involves an examination of their psychology and motivation. Viewed in this way, *A Passage to India* has a strong conventional plot. Adela Quested's arrival in India, her desire to see 'the *real* India', the expedition to the Marabar Caves, her accusation and the outcome at the trial, all follow a conventional pattern of setting a scene, bringing in complications that lead to a catastrophe and a final **dénouement** or resolution. When the novel is read in this manner, much of the narrative excitement fades once the trial scene is over and Adela leaves India. The conclusion of the 'Caves' section seems to be the true end of the novel and the 'Temple' section some kind of postscript bolted-on as an afterthought. Such a view would be understandable but excludes much of the subtlety of E.M. Forster's textual organisation. He found pleasure in conventional plotting but also recognised its limitations. He sought to overlay its rather constricting structures with a more open and expansive mode of organisation. As he writes in *Aspects of the Novel* (1927), written three years after this novel: 'Expansion. That is the idea that the novelist must cling to. Not completion. Not rounding off, but opening out'.

*A Passage to India* has a musical suggestiveness through its use of repeated images, phrases, and **plot motifs**. E.M. Forster called this technique 'rhythm' (see Language and Style) and felt that it gave novels a more integral, organic form. His own novel is cyclical as well as linear but this only becomes fully apparent in the final section. Only then do 'the soliciting images' of Mrs Moore and the wasp find their way back into Godbole's mystic trance as he seeks 'completeness not reconstruction' (Chapter 33, p. 259). As Aziz confronts Ralph in the Guest House at Mau and hears himself say 'Then you are an Oriental', the narrative turns back upon its itself in a mysterious manner: 'Mosque, caves, mosque, caves. And here he was starting again' (Chapter 36, p. 280). It is through such echoes and reverberations that a fiction of poetic suggestiveness emerges from a more time-driven novel of plot where 'the machinery ... will work to its end' (Chapter 22, p. 192).

# LANGUAGE AND STYLE

## THE USE OF THE OMNISCIENT NARRATOR

E.M. Forster uses a traditional method of telling his story that was much favoured by earlier novelists of the eighteenth and nineteenth centuries. It is that of an **omniscient narrator** who overviews the action, comments from any angle and can enter minds as dissimilar as Aziz's or Ronny Heaslop's. This narrator has a distinctive voice. He is humane, cultured, sceptical and **ironic**, but is also capable of modulating his voice to capture a tone of **lyrical** aspiration and wistful sadness. It is a voice, one imagines, not unlike E.M. Forster's own. A number of distinctive English, Anglo-Indian and Indian voices are dramatised within it, but it is this voice that dominates and prevails.

The omniscient narrator introduces and sets the tone for each section. He shapes and controls the direction of the text, mediating between the different racial groups and the interplay of different kinds of language. For example, the opening chapter gives us an overview of Chandrapore and its distinctive natural and social geography. Chapter 2 takes us into the Indian quarter where we listen to the colonised discussing their masters. Then we move on to the Civil Station, the mosque and the Club where we eavesdrop on the prejudiced opinions of the Anglo-Indians. The short Chapter 4 begins by noting the Indian response to the invitations to the Bridge-Party before the narrator pauses to give us a more extended meditation on the nature of invitations. By doing this, the narrator clearly underlines one of the **themes** that is central to the narrative.

Some of the complex modulations of language that E.M. Forster can achieve through this narrative device are apparent in the opening of Chapter 5. Ronny's callow platitudes about the guests at the other side of the tennis courts are followed by a silence:

> Some kites hovered overhead, impartial, over the kites passed the mass of a vulture, and with an impartiality exceeding all, the sky, not deeply coloured but translucent, poured light from its own circumference. It seemed unlikely that the series stopped here. Beyond the sky must not there be something that overarches all the skies, more impartial even than they? Beyond which again …

> They spoke of *Cousin Kate*. (p. 55)

The reader's eye and imagination are taken here from the deep human divide at ground level, through the predatory hierarchy of kites and vulture, to the 'overarching sky' introduced in Chapter 1 and then still further, before returning to earth abruptly in a shift that implies both comic **anticlimax** and something sadder, the limitations of the human spirit. Metaphysical speculation on a cosmic scale that exposes all human pretension gives way abruptly to the trivial social round once again. In such a manner, the omniscient narrator is constant presence in the text observing, judging, and commenting on the action. Chapters 1, 4, 10, 12, 23, 28 and 32 are almost entirely given up to the narrator and his speculative moralising, either directly in the manner of an essayist, or obliquely through the thoughts of his characters.

Through his running moral commentary, the narrator links and binds together the two distinct strands of **satirical** comedy and **lyrical** meditation that feature prominently in the text. The Club scene in Chapter 20 provides a good example of this. The 'crisis talk' of the Anglo-Indians is punctuated by the narrator's deflating **ironic** asides to great comic effect. Mrs Turton assumes 'her public safety voice' and towers protectively above the hapless Mrs Blakiston 'like Pallas Athene' (p. 172); 'At the name of Heaslop a fine and beautiful expression was renewed on very face' because 'he was bearing the sahib's cross' (p. 175). But a very different tone of bewildered sadness and regret emerges through Fielding's consciousness at the end of the chapter. Ejected roughly from the Club, he stands on the veranda and views the distant Marabar Hills that have caused all the trouble: 'At the moment they vanished they were everywhere, the cool benediction of the night descended, the stars sparkled, and the whole universe was a hill' (p. 179). This turn away from social drama or situational comedy into a mood of lyrical sadness or thoughtful melancholy at the end of chapters is characteristic. Good examples would be the end of Chapters 3, 7, 25, 26, 27 and 32.

It is the omniscient narrator who navigates the reader through their own 'passage to India' seeking, but unable to decipher, some of the contradictory messages of India's 'hundred voices', unable to decide whether India is a muddle or a mystery. As the text progresses the comic mimicry, the deflating asides, begin to fade and the tone of religious quest amplifies, but unlike his nineteenth-century precursors, E.M. Forster's controlling narrative voice does not provide much reassurance, only tentative questions. 'God si Love. Is this the final message of India?' (Chapter 33, p. 258).

## LANGUAGE BARRIERS

The omniscient narrator may have overall control but, within that voice, E.M. Forster dramatises many others. In doing so, he draws the reader's attention to the difficulties of communication; how language, especially in the colonial context, divides far more effectively than it unites. The voice of Anglo-India is that of a closely-knit group, confident and complacent. Mrs Turton, we are told, 'had learnt the lingo' but 'knew

none of the politer forms and of the verbs only the imperative mood'
(Chapter 5, p. 56). Through his mother's eyes we see Ronny's mouth
moving 'so complacently and competently beneath the little red nose'
repeating the appropriate clichés of the Club: 'We're out here to do justice
and keep the peace. Them's my sentiments. India isn't a drawing-room'
(Chapter 5, p. 62).

On the other side of the divide, the voice we hear most is that
of Aziz, an educated Moslem who works in the service of the Raj.
It is significant that quarrelling with Fielding at Mau he speaks
in Urdu 'so that the children might understand' (Chapter 35, p. 273)
for he mimes the language of 'the Ruling Race' for much of the
book: 'Slack Hindus – they have no ideas of society' (Chapter 7, p. 79);
'Well's here's luck! Chin-chin!' (Chapter 16, p. 152). Seeking to
ingratiate himself to the British, he becomes a **parody** of what he
most despises: 'Good bye, Miss Quested.' He pumped her hand up
and down to show that he felt at ease. 'You jolly jolly well not forget
those caves, won't you? I'll fix the whole show up in a jiffy' (Chapter 7,
p. 87).

E.M. Forster is sensitive to the mismatch that can occur between
what is intended and what is understood. At their first meeting, Aziz is
offended when Fielding disparages his remark about Post-
Impressionism, thinking that he is being scorned rather than the art
movement itself: 'a gulf divided his [Fielding's] remark from Mrs
Turton's "why they speak English", but to Aziz the two sounded alike'
(Chapter 7, p. 77).

This novel focuses on the difficulties of communication and the
failures of language. Frankness of speech, as Aziz warns Fielding
(Chapter 11), is dangerous in India. Conversation that should draw
people together all too often pulls them apart. Even Adela and Ronny
really have nothing to say to each other; it is the silent body contact in the
Nawab Bahadur's car that renews their engagement. Emotion and
language do not match. Indians cannot understand the cool logic of
the British – 'Is emotion a sack of potatoes, so much to the pound?'
(Chapter 27, p. 231) – and Aziz finds Fielding's confessions too
abstract: 'He liked confidences, however gross, but generalizations and
comparisons always repelled him. Life is not a scientific manual
(Chapter 31, p. 252). But Fielding finds Aziz's erotic references to female

breasts and disparaging remarks on Adela's physical appearance in 'bad taste' (Chapter 11, p. 120).

If Moslem and Christian find communication difficult, both flounder before the impenetrable evasiveness of Professor Godbole, the Brahmin Hindu.

> 'They are immensely holy, no doubt,' said Aziz, to help on the narrative.
> 'Oh no, oh no.'
> 'Still they are ornamental in some way.'
> 'Oh no.'
> 'Well, why are they so famous? We all talk of the famous Marabar Caves. Perhaps that is an empty brag.'
> 'No, I should not quite say that.' (Chapter 7, p. 84)

Aziz will not discover what is so 'extraordinary' about the Marabar Caves. Engaging with Godbole is 'encountering Ancient Night' (Chapter 7, p. 84). Nor will the anxious Fielding get a straight answer to his question: 'Is Aziz innocent or guilty?' (Chapter 19, p. 168). 'Nothing embraces the whole of India, nothing, nothing' (Chapter 14, p. 142); least of all language.

## RHYTHM: THE USE OF REPEATED IMAGES, PHRASES AND MOTIFS

E.M. Forster drew many of his analogies for the writing process from music, and it is helpful to think of *A Passage to India* as a symphonic structure with its three sections as 'movements', each with its distinctive texture and verbal tone. For example, certain elemental and seasonal images dominate in each of the three sections: the Indian spring and moon in 'Mosque', high summer, sun and the Indian earth in 'Caves', water and the rainy monsoon season in 'Temple' (see Narrative Techniques and Structure).

However, although the **imagery** in each section has a distinctive bias, E.M. Forster also orchestrates his language in an attempt to relate the sections to each other and to shape the novel overall. He does this by a method of repetition and variation of words, phrases, key images and larger plot **motifs** that, noting its use by other novelists in *Aspects of the Novel* (1927), he termed 'rhythm'. He observed there that it is by use of this method that apparently shapeless novels are 'stitched internally'. A motif is a repeated feature in music, literature or the visual arts that recurs for a significant effect. A more specialised term borrowed from music is **leitmotif** which is a repeated musical phrase that gathers meaning and significance each time it recurs.

Examples of this technique in *A Passage to India* include the repetition of key words and phrases like 'extraordinary' (Chapter 1, pp. 29–30; Chapter 7, p. 84; Chapter 12, p. 126), 'nothing' (Chapter 12, p. 126; Chapter 14, pp. 139, 142, 146; Chapter 20, p. 179), 'the overarching sky' (Chapter 1, p. 30; Chapter 5, pp. 55, 64–5; Chapter 37, p. 289), 'mystery' and 'muddle' (see Recurring Themes). There is also a distinctive pattern of words in duplicate or triplicate that repeat or echo one another like 'come, come, come' (Chapter 8, p. 87; Chapter 8, p. 93; Chapter 14, p. 136; Chapter 19, p. 169; Chapter 33, p. 263), 'pomper, pomper, pomper' (Chapter 14, p. 135), 'weak, weak, weak' (Chapter 20, p. 179; Chapter 24, p. 200), 'kindness, more kindness, and even after that more kindness' (Chapter 11, p. 118; Chapter 26, p. 223), 'good will, and more good will and more good will' (Chapter 5, p. 64). The echo motif from the Marabar Caves is elaborately instigated in Chapter 14 and then its undermining significance spreads outward from Mrs Moore's disorientating experience at the end of that chapter throughout the rest of the 'Caves' section (see Symbolism). The image of the snake that proves to be a tree-stump on the journey to the Caves is taken up by the 'coiling worms' of the Caves's echoes (Chapter 14, pp. 139, 144), the Russell's viper in the Government College (Chapter 19. p. 167) and the 'undying worm' of Mrs Moore's disillusion (Chapter 23, p. 194). An apparently insignificant detail like the wasp (Chapter 3, p. 50; Chapter 4, p. 53) gains immense significance by its reappearance much later in Chapter 33 (p. 263), as does the phrase 'Then you are an Oriental' (Chapter 2, p. 41; Chapter 36, p. 280). There are other oddly distorted but healing echoes: 'God ... is ... Love' (Chapter 5, p. 64) becomes 'God si Love' (Chapter 33, p. 258; Chapter 36, p. 284), and the 'Esmiss Esmoor' chant at the trial (Chapter 24, p. 207), returns to merge with 'the repeating and inverting' of other Hindu deities and haunt Aziz at Mau (Chapter 36, p. 282). Professor's Godbole's call to Krishna (Chapter 7, p. 87) is **parodied** by Ronny's demand for his servant Krishna (Chapter 8, p. 101), and the mysterious car accident in Chapter 8 that brings Adela and Ronny together again prefigures the events at the Caves later that tear them apart. E.M. Forster's use of this technique helps to give the narrative a meaningful texture and density, foregrounding important themes, developing arguments and suggesting complex ideas.

## THE SYMBOLISM OF THE MARABAR CAVES

The Marabar Caves are at the heart of *A Passage to India*, both literarily, structurally and **symbolically**. In his 1952 interview E.M. Forster said that they 'represented an area in which concentration can take place. A cavity. They were something to focus everything up: they were to engender an event like an egg'. In terms of **plot** they play a crucial role: Adela's quest for 'the *real* India' leads inexorably to the Caves, the panic they engender and the working though of some dismaying consequences. Aziz is imprisoned and tried, Mrs Moore dies on her early journey home, Adela's engagement is broken off, and the friendship between Aziz and Fielding falters.

But the Marabar Hills and their 'extraordinary' Caves function as a focus for several of the novel's **themes** as well as being a plot device. In this respect, they possess a powerful symbolic force and resonance. They make their appearance in the opening sentence of the novel, and their menacing 'fists and fingers' 'thrust up' through the soil at the end of the first chapter suggest the disturbing presence of an incomplete burial or a disturbed grave that threatens the tidy monotony of the Civil Station (Chapter 1, p. 30). They are the most frightening, manifestation of the hostility of the Indian earth to European power and control. Chapter 12 develops their **anthropomorphic** imagery on a grand scale. If 'flesh of the sun's flesh is to be touched anywhere, it is here, among the incredible antiquity of these hills' (p. 125). This idea of the Hills and Caves as prehistoric and impervious to all human culture is stressed as the picnic expedition approaches them in Chapter 14: 'Before man with his itch for the seemly, had been born, the planet must have looked thus' (p. 144).

Like all successful symbols, there is much in the presentation of the Marabar Hills and their Caves that is ambivalent. They can be both beautiful and terrible. From the outside, the Caves are uninviting but their inner skin is 'smoother than windless water, more voluptuous than love' (Chapter 12, p. 126). 'Nothing, nothing attaches to them', 'Nothing is inside them', they add 'nothing ... to sum of good and evil'

(Chapter 12, pp. 126–7) yet it is this nothingness that makes them 'extraordinary'. In themselves, the Caves seem neutral, sterile even, for the splendid revelations in their polished inner surfaces can only be revealed by the flames brought inside by human agency and when the flames die, they die also. Similarly their sinister echo can only be released by the human voice. Their principle challenge seems to lie in their capacity to amplify whatever is brought into them until it cannot be repressed.

The Marabar Hills and Caves are especially resistant to all attempts at expropriation and representation through culture and language. "Bou-oum", or "ou-boum", – utterly dull' (Chapter 14, p. 144), but 'nothing' becomes 'something' when Mrs Moore goes into the cave and its echo exposes the pretensions of her 'poor little talkative Christianity' (p. 146). For her, the challenge is a spiritual one and the echo 'undermines her hold on life'. She likes mysteries but she 'rather dislikes muddles' (see Chapter 7, p. 79) and the Marabar Hills and Caves appear to be a metaphysical muddle on the grandest scale.

For Adela, the challenge seems more psychological; the Caves expose her barren emotional life and fear of the physical. As she contemplates the distant beauty of the hills at the Bridge-Party, a vision of her married life falls 'like a shutter' (Chapter 5, p. 60). Such repression will have consequences that extend far beyond herself. The Caves temporarily break the power of reason in her, reducing her to mental and bodily breakdown.

'Yet absence implies presence, absence is not non-existence' as Godbole informs the distraught Fielding (Chapter 19, p. 169); the undermining echo and the infinite void of the Caves do not have the last word. They activate all the racial hostility in Chandrapore and for a while seem invincible but Mrs Moore's death and Adela's recantation have something sacrificial in them that weakens their power. By the end of the novel, their echoes have faded, become less insistent. They have become just one more of 'the hundred voices of India', drawn into a grander cycle of spiritual loss and gain: 'Infinite Love took upon itself the form of SHRI KRISHNA, and saved the world. All sorrow was annihilated, not only for Indians, but foreigners, birds, caves, railways, and the stars' (Chapter 33, p. 260).

# PART FOUR

# TEXTUAL ANALYSIS

### TEXT 1    (CHAPTER 3, PP. 48–9)

Their attention was diverted. Below them a radiance had suddenly appeared. It belonged neither to water nor moonlight, but stood like a luminous sheaf upon the fields of darkness. He told them that it was where the new sandbank was forming, and that the dark ravelled bit at the top was the sand, and that the dead bodies floated down that way from Benares, or would if the crocodiles let them. 'It's not much of a dead body that gets down to Chandrapore.'

'Crocodiles down in it too, how terrible!' his mother murmured. The young people glanced at each other and smiled; it amused them when the old lady got these gentle creeps, and harmony was restored between them consequently. She continued: 'What a terrible river! What a wonderful river!' and sighed. The radiance was already altering, whether through shifting of the moon or of the sand; soon the bright sheaf would be gone, and a circlet, itself to alter, be burnished upon the streaming void. The women discussed whether they would wait for the change or not, while the silence broke into patches of unquietness and the mare shivered. On her account they did not wait, but drove on to the City Magistrate's bungalow, where Miss Quested went to bed, and Mrs Moore had a short interview with her son.

He wanted to inquire about the Mohammedan doctor in the mosque. It was his duty to report suspicious characters, and conceivably it was some disreputable hakim who had prowled up from the bazaar. When she told him that it was someone connected with the Minto Hospital, he was relieved, and said that the fellow's name must be Aziz, and that he was quite all right, nothing against him at all.

'Aziz! What a charming name!'

'So you and he had a talk. Did you gather he was well-disposed?'

Ignorant of the force of this question, she replied, 'Yes, quite, after the first moment.'

'I meant, generally. Did he seem to tolerate us – the brutal conqueror, the sun-dried bureaucrat, that sort of thing?'

'Oh yes, I think so, except the Callendars – he doesn't care for the Callendars at all.'

'Oh. So he told you that, did he? The Major will be interested. I wonder what was the aim of the remark.'

'Ronny, Ronny! You're never going to pass it on to Major Callendar?'

'Yes, rather. I must, in fact!'

'But, my dear boy –'

'If the Major heard I was disliked by any native subordinate of mine, I should expect him to pass it on to me.'

'But, my dear boy – a private conversation!'

'Nothing's private in India. Aziz knew that when he spoke out, so don't you worry. He had some motive in what he said. My personal belief is that the remark wasn't true.'

'How not true?'

'He abused the Major in order to impress you.'

'I don't know what you mean, dear.'

'It's the educated native's latest dodge. They used to cringe, but the younger generation believe in a show of manly independence. They think it will pay better with the itinerant M.P. But whether the native swaggers or cringes, there's always something behind every remark he makes, always something, and if nothing else he's trying to increase his izzat – in plain Anglo-Saxon, to score. Of course there are exceptions.'

'You never used to judge people like this at home.'

This passage is taken from the early stages of the 'Mosque' section and, characteristically, is a night scene dominated by the powerful Indian moon. Mrs Moore and Adela are returning to Ronny's bungalow after an evening at the Club. Leaving during the interval of *Cousin Kate*, Mrs Moore has met Aziz, by chance, at the mosque. While Adela has complained of not seeing 'the *real* India', Mrs Moore has unwittingly followed Fielding's advice, 'Try seeing Indians' (p. 44), much to Ronny's annoyance. Tension between him and Adela is already becoming evident as she is showing some alarmingly independent views on 'the native question' (p. 48).

The passage opens with a description of the Ganges at night. We have been prepared for this in Chapter 1 where the **omniscient narrator** has mapped out the setting and geography of Chandrapore. We are told there that the river 'happens not to be holy here' but 'Houses do fall, people are drowned and left rotting' (p. 29). This passage continues to develop the idea of India's deceptive qualities from the opening chapter. The river is the sordid conveyer of dead bodies from the holy centre of Benares, 'or would if the crocodiles let them', but here it is transformed by the moon's reflection into a scene of enchanting beauty.

Earlier 'A sudden sense of unity, of kinship with the heavenly bodies' (p. 46) had passed through Mrs Moore and it is her response that is given here and seems appropriate to the potent magic of the scene: 'What a terrible river! What a wonderful river!' The narrator has informed us at the beginning of this chapter that in India 'Adventures do occur, but not punctually' (p. 43) and this moment of transient beauty as the moon plays on the shifting sandbank may be compared to the disappointment of the false dawn as the picnic party travels to the Marabar Hills (Chapter 14, pp. 136–7).

The first part of the passage is narrated by the omniscient narrator and the speech of Mrs Moore and her son are embedded or reported within it. The non-verbal communication between Adela and Ronny is observed by the narrator and anticipates events in the car in Chapter 8. It is the narrator who gives us the poetic impression of the scene through the use of a lyrical **simile** and **metaphors** that makes striking links between the concrete and the abstract: 'like a luminous sheaf on the field of darkness', 'the bright sheaf', 'burnished on the streaming void', 'patches of unquietness'.

The second half of the passage moves on to a new scene, a **dialogue** between Mrs Moore and her son on their return to the bungalow. There is a transition to a more dramatic representation of character where readers have to make their own judgements and draw their own conclusions. This transition is smoothly directed through a paragraph of **free indirect style** where Ronny's opening remarks to his mother are reported through the narrator. The paragraph is flavoured by Ronny's bureaucratic officiousness, racist language, and Anglo-Indian Club talk:

'duty to report', 'disreputable hakim', 'prowled up from the bazaar', 'fellow's name', 'quite all right' and 'nothing against him'.

Ronny is the City Magistrate and this conversation has something of an official interrogation about it. It reveals the suspicion and insecurity of the Anglo-Indian community. Earlier in this chapter we have learnt that 'Heaslop's a sahib; he's the type we want, he's one of us' (p. 43) and his conversation is full of clichés promoting the cynicism of his elders. These are often introduced with the definite article to increase their generalising power and invest them with bogus authority: 'the brutal conqueror, the sun-dried bureaucrat', 'the educated native's latest dodge', 'whether the native swaggers or cringes', 'the itinerant M.P'. We learn subsequently that 'of course there are exceptions' and 'increasing the izzat' are phrases he has learnt from Turton and Callendar. His willingness to betray private confidences in the cause of race solidarity anticipates McBryde's assertion later that 'The man who doesn't toe the line is lost' (Chapter 18, p. 164) for he leaves a gap and weakens his friends.

'Nothing's private in India' – Despite his show of confidence, Ronny is actually as wrong here as he is in Chapter 8 when he declares that Aziz's missing collar stud shows 'the fundamental slackness that reveals the race' (p. 89). We know through the omnipresence of the narrator in the previous chapter that Aziz had no ulterior motive in opening his heart to Mrs Moore. In the concluding part of this chapter, Mrs Moore is left to retire for the night and consider her son's biased interpretation of Aziz's behaviour at the mosque. 'Yes, it was all true, but how false as a summary of the man; the essential life of him had been slain' (p. 50). It is in this mood that she empathises with the wasp, the 'Pretty dear' who similarly disregards the barriers of outside and inside, and doesn't know its place.

TEXT $2$    (CHAPTER 14, PP. 143–4)

> The first cave was tolerably convenient. They skirted the puddle of water, and then climbed up over some unattractive stones, the sun crashing on their backs. Bending their heads, they disappeared one by one into the interior of the hills. The small black hole gaped where their varied forms and colours had momentarily functioned. They were sucked in like water down a drain. Bland and bald rose the

precipices; bland and glutinous the sky that connected the precipices; solid and white, a Brahmany kite flapped between the rocks with a clumsiness that seemed intentional. Before man, with his itch for the seemly, had been born, the planet must have looked thus. The kite flapped away ... Before birds, perhaps ... And then the hole belched and humanity returned.

A Marabar cave had been horrid as far as Mrs Moore was concerned, for she had nearly fainted in it, and had some difficulty in preventing herself from saying so as soon as she got into the air again. It was natural enough; she had always suffered from faintness, and the cave had become too full, because all their retinue followed them. Crammed with villagers and servants, the circular chamber began to smell. She lost Aziz and Adela in the dark, didn't know who touched her, couldn't breathe, and some vile naked thing struck her face and settled on her mouth like a pad. She tried to regain the entrance tunnel, but an influx of villagers swept her back. She hit her head. For an instant she went mad, hitting and gasping like a fanatic. For not only did the crush and stench alarm her; there was also a terrifying echo.

Professor Godbole had never mentioned an echo; it never impressed him, perhaps. There are some exquisite echoes in India; there is the whisper round the dome at Bijapur; there are the long, solid sentences that voyage through the air at Mandu, and return unbroken to their creator. The echo in a Marabar cave is not like these, it is entirely devoid of distinction. Whatever is said, the same monotonous noise replies, and quivers up and down the walls until it is absorbed into the roof. 'Boum' is the sound as far as the human alphabet can express it, or 'bou-oum', or 'ou-boum' – utterly dull. Hope, politeness, the blowing of a nose, the squeak of a boot, all produce 'boum'. Even the striking of a match starts a little worm coiling, which is too small to complete a circle, but is eternally watchful. And if several people talk at once, an overlapping howling noise begins, echoes generate echoes, and the cave is stuffed with a snake composed of small snakes, which writhe independently.

After Mrs Moore all the others poured out. She had given the signal for the reflux. Aziz and Adela both emerged smiling and she did not want him to think his treat was a failure, so smiled too. As each person emerged she looked for a villain, but none was there, and she realised that she had been among the mildest individuals, whose only desire was to honour her, and that the naked pad was a poor little baby, astride its mother's hips. Nothing evil had been in the cave, but she had not enjoyed herself; no, she had not enjoyed herself, and she decided not to visit a second one.

This passage is taken from the visit to the Marabar Caves which is the central episode of the 'Caves' section and a critical one for the novel as a whole. After the arrival of the party and the taking of some refreshment, Aziz has told the English ladies stories of the great Mogul Emperors, but Adela's anxiety about her 'Anglo-Indian difficulty' (p. 143) has broken the mood. Reluctantly they begin their sightseeing.

In the first paragraph we observe events from the **point of view** of the **omniscient narrator** who watches the party enter the cave. The tone is fastidious, even dismissive, to begin with. The cave is 'tolerably convenient' and the stones 'unattractive'. The sun dominates 'crashing on' their backs with the **metaphorical** weight of a physical force. The language becomes progressively more sinister as the paragraph develops. This effect is partially achieved through the use of **anthropomorphic** imagery. The hills are like a giant body, an idea already developed through the repeated **motif** of their 'fists and fingers' that 'thrust up through the soil' at the end of the first chapter (p. 30) and the extended description we have of them in Chapter 12. The use of metaphors here continue to give added emphasis to this notion. The cave entrances 'gape', the visitors are 'sucked in' and 'belched' out again.

The 'incredible antiquity' (p. 125) of the Marabar Hills stressed in Chapter 12 is further underlined in this passage and adds to the sense of foreboding. Once the visitors have disappeared into the cave taking all traces of human activity with them, the empty scene becomes eerily prehistoric. The rocks, stripped of any distinguishing marks, are 'bland' and 'bald'. The sky is 'glutinous'. Sticking to the earth, it is quite unlike the 'overarching sky' of the opening chapter and anticipates the claustrophobia that drives Mrs Moore out of the cave. The only animate object in the scene is the Brahmany kite. Its clumsiness as it flies away makes it more akin to a pterodactyl than a bird: 'Before man, with his itch for the seemly, had been born, the planet must have looked thus'. Here, the 'seemly', the desire for a human scale, is no longer the norm. It is a temporary aberration like an 'itch'. The use of **ellipsis** to break up the sentences at the end of the paragraph suggests a mind meditating but reluctant to come to conclusions.

In the next paragraph, the viewpoint changes and we experience the inside of the cave from Mrs Moore's point of view. The emphasis is on repulsive physical contact, a sense of suffocation and a feeling of disgust.

Experiencing the '*real*' India is like being absorbed into the stomach or gut of an alien body. The cave is 'horrid'. It 'begins to smell'. Undifferentiated Indian humanity overwhelms her, causing her to panic. In the 'crush' and 'stench', the physical confines of the cave become indistinguishable from its inhabitants. An unspecified 'vile naked thing' threatens to choke her and, in her fight for air, she loses her dignity. Cultural and racial distinctions collapse as an elderly English lady becomes 'a fanatic'. We experience here through Mrs Moore what we can only surmise of Adela's hysteria, physical revulsion and flight from the Kawa Dol later.

With the mention of the 'terrifying echo', physical panic gives way to spiritual menace. We move back to the more detached, contemplative style of the narrator for the discussion of the echo which is to have such a central **symbolic** significance for the rest of the novel. The narrator's **persona** is that of the knowledgeable Indian traveller who introduces us to Chandrapore in Chapter 1 and to the Marabar Caves in Chapter 12. He has experienced the 'whispers' of Bijapur and the more substantial echoes of Mandu for himself and so can vouch for the dullness of the Marabar's 'monotonous noise'.

'Boum', 'bou-oum', 'ou-boom': the sounds resist representation in the any human language. It is possible to hear in them either some indecipherable sacred mystery, or the emptiness of nihilistic despair. They undermine all attempts to impose meaning on the world and dissolve all distinguishing features into the same sound. The noblest aspirations or the most trivial noise just produce 'boum'. The narrator measures the scale from 'Hope' to 'the squeak of a boot'. Of all the many voices of India, these are the most unintelligible. They may express mystery – or only muddle.

The symbolism of the snakes is similarly ambiguous. In the world's religions the snake can signify both wisdom and evil. Eternity can be symbolised as a snake devouring its own tail. Here 'the little worm' of an echo roused by the noise of a match striking is 'too small to complete a circle'. The **imagery** of 'echoes generating echoes' and of a snake composed of smaller snakes 'writhing independently' gives a sense of perverse alien life and corruption that is hostile to human existence. From the start, the Marabar has been associated with danger and poison. Aziz warns Mrs Moore that snakes from the hills threaten Chandrapore at their first meeting in Chapter 2 (p. 39). (For further discussion of the snake imagery see the commentary on Chapters 19, 23 and the section on 'rhythm' in Language and Style.)

The stress on the smallness of the snakes here, and later, when the narrator talks of 'the serpent of eternity made of maggots' and the 'undying worm' that is 'snub-nosed, incapable of generosity' (Chapter 23, p. 194), suggest that it is the pettiness of evil and the triviality of human egotism that is being stressed here. The claustrophobia that the Caves induce is spiritual as well as physical. They 'robbed infinity and eternity of their vastness (p. 146). In a more psychological sense, snake imagery is also suggestively sexual, and this may have relevance to Adela's reactions later.

The last paragraph returns us to the social world and Mrs Moore's perspective once again. She realises that the dehumanised 'pad' that threatened to smother her was 'a poor little baby' and the press of stinking flesh only a crowd of benign well-wishers. However, despite this recognition of normal humanity and a return to social obligation as she attempts to conceal her discomfort, the paragraph ends in a cluster of negatives. That Mrs Moore has been fatally undermined by 'the twilight of the double vision' (Chapter 23, p. 193) is evident by the end of the chapter, and she will never recover.

## TEXT 3     (CHAPTER 36, PP. 279–80)

'You should not treat us like this,' he challenged, and this time Aziz was checked, for the voice, though frightened, was not weak.

'Like what?'

'Dr Aziz, we have done you no harm.'

'Aha, you know my name, I see. Yes, I am Aziz. No, of course your great friend Miss Quested did me no harm at the Marabar.'

Drowning his last words, all the guns of the State went off. A rocket from the jail garden gave the signal. The prisoner had been released, and was kissing the feet of the singers. Rose-leaves fall from the houses, sacred spices and coconut are brought forth ... It was the halfway moment; the God had extended His temple, and paused exultantly. Mixed and confused in their passage, the rumours of salvation entered the Guest House. They were startled and moved onto the porch, drawn by the sudden illumination. The bronze gun up on the fort kept flashing, the town was a blur of light, in which the house seemed dancing, and the palace waving little wings. The water below, the hills and sky above, were not involved as yet; there was still only a little light and song struggling among the shapeless lumps of the universe. The song became audible through much repetition; the choir was repeating and inverting the names of deities.

'Radhakrishna, Radhakrishna,
Radhakrishna, Radhakrishna,
Krishnaradha, Radhakrishna,
Radhakrishna, Radhakrishna,'

they sang, and woke the sleeping sentry in the Guest House; he leant upon his iron-tipped spear.

'I must go back now, good night,' said Aziz, and held out his hand, completely forgetting that they were not friends, and focusing his heart on something more distant than the caves, something beautiful. His hand was taken, and then he remembered how detestable he had been, and said gently, 'Don't you think me unkind any more?'

'No.'

'How can you tell, you strange fellow?'

'Not difficult, the one thing I always know.'

'Can you always tell whether a stranger is your friend?'

'Yes.'

'Then you are an Oriental.' He unclasped as he spoke, with a little shudder. Those words – he had said them to Mrs Moore in the mosque at the beginning of the cycle, from which, after so much suffering, he had got free. Never be friends with the English! Mosque, caves, mosque, caves. And here he was starting again. He handed the magic ointment to him. 'Take this, think of me when you use it. I shall never want it back. I must give you one little present, and it is all I have got; you are Mrs Moore's son.'

'I am that,' he murmured to himself; and a part of Aziz's mind that had been hidden seemed to move and force its way to the top.

'But you are Heaslop's brother also, and alas, the two nations cannot be friends.'

'I know. Not yet.'

'Did your mother speak to you about me?'

'Yes.' And with a swerve of the voice and body that Aziz did not follow he added: 'In her letters, in her letters. She loved you.'

'Yes, your mother was my best friend in all the world.' He was silent, puzzled by his own great gratitude. What did this eternal goodness of Mrs Moore amount to? To nothing, if brought to the test of thought. She had not borne witness in his favour, nor visited him in the prison, yet she had stolen to the depths of his heart, and he always adored her.

This passage is taken from 'Temple', the final section of the novel, where Aziz visits the State Guest House with some ointment for Ralph Moore's bee stings. Actually, he has assumed the place to be empty because on his ride over he has seen a boat on the lake. The ointment is an excuse. His real purpose is to spy and satisfy his curiosity about the English visitors. He is reading private letters in a bitter state of mind when he is surprised by Ralph Moore who has stayed behind alone. His treatment of Ralph is unsympathetic and this passage opens with Ralph's reproof.

There is a mixture of **dialogue** and the use of the **omniscient narrator** here. Sometimes the narrator describes comments on events from a commanding position, sometimes he limits himself to Aziz's consciousness. At no point do we enter Ralph Moore's consciousness. We see him only from Aziz's **point of view,** and this has the effect of making him rather mysterious and unknowable.

At Aziz's mention of the Marabar, speech is 'drowned' by the rejoicing of the festival. This is a clichéd expression normally but may have some genuine **metaphorical** significance here as water imagery is prevalent in this section and suggestive of healing properties. The paragraph describing the religious celebrations is highly figurative in its use of language as the narrator attempts to give us a sense of religious ecstasy and release. The salute of the guns and the rocket mime the release of the prisoner and this, in turn, seems to mime Aziz's release from the resentments of the past. The narrator's point of view is very mobile and the prose very impressionistic. We move from the sight of the grateful convict to an overview of the celebrations in the town, and then finally to a more distanced perspective from the porch of the Guest House over the lake.

Physical details like the prostrate prisoner kissing the feet of the singers, the falling rose-leaves, the spices and coconut, the flashing gun at the fort, are mixed with more general commentary: 'It was the half-way moment; the God had extended His temple' and 'rumours of salvation entered the Guest House'. The language and imagery are exotic, and phrases like 'brought forth', 'extended His temple', 'paused exultantly', are biblical, suggesting religious joy and transformation.

The metaphorical expressions are striking, mixing abstract and concrete, spiritual and commonplace: 'the God had extended His temple, and paused exultantly'; 'rumours of salvation'; 'the town was a blur of light'; 'shapeless lumps of the universe'. The suggestion that all the elements in the world are responding to events in joyous accord is aided by the prevalent use of **personification** in this first long paragraph. Guns go off, rose-leaves fall from houses, sacred spices and coconut are brought forth, rumours of salvation enter the Guest House, houses dance and the palace waves little wings, light and song struggle, even water, hill and sky are waiting to be involved, without any obvious human agency.

The chanting of male and female Hindu deities, interchanged and mixed together, suggests the inclusiveness of Hinduism just as the release of the prisoner is a ritual drawn from the actions of a Moslem saint long ago. The chant itself is an echo, benevolent and healing, of the earlier 'Esmiss Esmoor' heard during the trial scene' (Chapter 24, p. 207). Aziz recalls 'the syllables of salvation' later in this chapter (p. 282).

'God is here' – the exchange between Aziz and Ralph Moore is a recapitulation of the earlier meeting between Aziz and Mrs Moore in the mosque (Chapter 2, pp. 38–41) but now in a different religious context. This is the memory 'more distant than the caves, something beautiful' and a good example of E.M. Forster's use of 'rhythm' (see Language and Style). It demonstrates repetition of a plot **motif** with significant variation. Ralph knows whether a stranger is a friend, just as his mother knew whether she liked or disliked people. Aziz's response to them both is the same: 'Then you are an Oriental'.

The repetition of this statement (see p. 41) is another echo which brings events full circle to 'the beginning of the cycle': 'Mosque, caves, mosque, caves. And here he was starting again'. After so much suffering,

Aziz, like the prisoner, has become free but only to become, once more, drawn into a relationship across the racial divide. The gift of the ointment to soothe Ralph's bee stings is a tacit acknowledgement of this. Even in the reason for the visit Mrs Moore's influence is still at work. At their first meeting in Chapter 2, Aziz and Mrs Moore joke about snakes and he mentions a six spot beetle: 'you pick it up, it bites, you die' (p. 40). Later that evening at the end of the following chapter, Mrs Moore contemplates a sleeping wasp (p. 50). During Godbole's reverie in Chapter 33 that introduces this section, Mrs Moore comes into his mind linked to a wasp (p. 259). Such small details, apparently random, build up into an image cluster that associates Mrs Moore with poisonous insects. The effect of this is to suggest that her influence is still at work over Ralph's mishap with the bees, drawing the two men together.

During their first conversation in the mosque, Mrs Moore discussed her two families with Aziz, and now the topic returns to underline the divisions between the two nations. Ralph and Ronny have come to symbolise the private and the public life. Connections and ties of a personal nature cannot be reproduced at a political and national level. If Ralph has the sensitivity and intuition that make friendship possible, Ronny represents the officialdom of Empire that makes such bonds across the racial divide impossible; at least 'not yet', and the implied hope in the phrase is repeated in the final sentence of the novel (p. 289).

The passage ends with Aziz considering the power of intuition and emotion over reason. In Chapter 27, Fielding had questioned his irrational devotion to Mrs Moore as he does himself now, and his response had been: 'Is emotion a sack of potatoes, so much to the pound, to be measured out? (p. 231). 'The secret understanding of the heart' (Chapter 2, p. 38) is unreasonable, and therein lies its value and significance.

Aziz's softening to Ralph here is one of three moments of reconciliation and harmony that form the complicated **closure** of the novel. It follows the mystical reappearance and acceptance of Mrs Moore as a memory in Godbole's trance (Chapter 33, p. 259), and anticipates the truce between Aziz and Fielding in the final chapter.

# PART FIVE

# BACKGROUND

## THE AUTHOR AND HIS WORK

E.M. Forster was born in 1879 into a cultured upper-middle-class family, but his father, an architect, died the following year. His early childhood was spent in the caring, protective company of three women: his mother, maternal grandmother and his great aunt, Marianne Thorton, who was to exert the greatest influence on his life. She died when he was eight leaving him a legacy of £8,000 for which he was forever grateful. It enabled him to lead a life of private means and become a writer. The Thortons were originally members of an influential group of metropolitan evangelicals active in the late eighteenth and nineteenth centuries called 'The Clapham Sect'. E.M. Forster became very conscious of this ancestry which seems to have left its influence in his judgemental attitudes and moral seriousness.

After a happy early childhood, much of it spent at 'Rooksnest', an unpretentious country home near Stevenage in Hertfordshire and the original 'Howards End' in his novel of that name, the family moved to Tonbridge so that the young E.M. Forster could attend the Public School there as a day-boy. Tonbridge is the original for 'Sawston', E.M. Forster's fictional home counties suburbia and symbol for an unrelenting small-minded respectability satirised in his early novels. E.M. Forster was not happy at Tonbridge and later attacked English Public Schools for producing boys who had 'undeveloped hearts'. Matters improved considerably when he went to King's College, Cambridge. He counted the years 1897–1901 spent as an undergraduate there as among the happiest in his life. It was at Cambridge that he came under the influence of the moral philosopher, G.E. Moore, who stressed the importance of personal relationships and the power of art to influence life for the good.

E.M. Forster had been attracted by the classical ideals while at Cambridge. He became a sceptical humanist agnostic who believed that the fulfilled life lay in finding a balance between body and mind. He spent the next few years travelling, mostly in the ancient classical world, writing and teaching. It was through tutoring Latin for university entrance exams that he met Syed Masood, the original for Aziz, in 1906. *A Passage to India* is dedicated to him and it was through him that E.M. Forster developed his life-long interest in India. He visited Masood on his visit to India in 1912–13 and, encouraged by him, began his first draft of the novel.

E.M. Forster published four novels in the first decade of the twentieth century, *Where Angels Fear to Tread* (1905), *The Longest Journey* (1907), *A Room with a View* (1908), and *Howards End* (1910). The grace and skill in which he attacked English middle-class complacency and insularity in these novels has led to frequent comparison with Jane Austen, but he also shows a yearning aspiration for individual fulfilment that is all his own. *Howards End* is the most complex and ambitious of these novels where E.M. Forster sought to articulate the growing sense of national crisis in the years leading up to the First World War.

E.M. Forster spent much of the war years as a Red Cross worker in Egypt. It was here, in Alexandria, that he had his first happy, sexual relationship with Mohammed el Adl, an Egyptian tram-conductor, and began to come to terms with his sexuality. Just before the war he had begun a novel of homosexual love called *Maurice*, but this remained unpublished during his lifetime. After a second visit to India in 1921–2, he finally completed and published *A Passage to India* in 1924; it was to be his last novel.

E.M. Forster developed a new career as journalist, essayist, broadcaster, academic and public figure. In his private life he found happiness when his meeting with a young policeman, Bob Buckingham, in 1929, led to a lasting companionship. He continued to publish a wide variety of books including a critical work, *Aspects of the Novel* (1927), two collections of essays, *Abinger Harvest* (1936) and *Two Cheers for Democracy* (1951), and a book on his Indian travels called *The Hill of Devi* (1953). During and after the Second World War, he became a revered figure of sanity and humane values who celebrated the virtues of the private life during the fight against fascism and, later, totalitarian communism. In 1945 he was elected Honorary Fellow at King's College, Cambridge where he settled for the rest of his long life. He died in 1970. *Maurice* (1971) and *The Life to Come* (1972), a collection of homosexual short stories, were published posthumously.

E.M. Forster was born into a world of culture and some affluence. He once famously observed that he belonged to 'the fag-end of Victorian liberalism'. Apart from *A Passage to India*, all his novels were written before 1914 and celebrate an Edwardian world of unrivalled middle-class stability and prosperity that was swept away by the First World War. Of course, life for the majority was very far from stable or prosperous: industrial capitalism at home and Imperialism overseas made wealth for the few at the expense of the many. Laissez-faire economics and the unfettered freedom of the individual are classic liberal beliefs but poverty and urban squalor touched the conscience of liberal intellectuals and politicians, leading to the great reforming Liberal administration of 1906–11. E.M. Forster's writings demonstrate this split and crisis in liberalism, the so-called 'liberal dilemma'. He sought to preserve and continue the great cultural tradition of the Victorian elite while criticising the unjust economic and social system that sustained it. This led to an unresolvable tension in his texts between satirical observations of middle-class life as it was, and Utopian yearnings for a more fulfilling future in a less industrialised world.

E.M. Forster's homosexuality was an additional complicating factor that had to be coded into his texts as a hidden agenda. The Labouchère amendment to the Criminal Law Amendment Act of 1885, making homosexual acts in private a crime, followed by the notorious Oscar Wilde trials in 1895, made it difficult for E.M. Forster to write and publish freely about issues that concerned him greatly. This was almost certainly a factor that contributed to his literary silence after *A Passage to India*.

While at Cambridge, E.M. Forster was invited to join an exclusive debating society called 'the Apostles'. Other members included the economist, Maynard Keynes, the art critic Roger Fry, Leonard Woolf, future husband of the novelist Virginia Woolf, and the biographer Lytton Strachey. This club became the nucleus of the Bloomsbury Group, an informal association of writers, artists, painters, critics and thinkers that was influential in the artistic and intellectual life of London in the years leading up to the First World War. E.M. Forster was never a central figure in the group, but its social and intellectual support helped him to maintain his artistic purpose and its scorn for complacent middle-class convention is apparent in his own writing. Like them, he celebrated love, friendship, art and the importance of the private life over the power of bureaucracy, Imperialism and the exercise of public power.

*A Passage to India* is, in many ways, a conventional novel. E.M. Forster's roots as a writer of fiction lay in the great tradition of nineteenth-century **realism**. Such fictions have a commanding first or third person narrator who overviews the action, a strong plot to sustain narrative interest, and coherently presented characters who have to interact with a society that is closely observed, and whose choices have clear moral consequences. Some of E.M. Forster's older contemporaries like John Galsworthy and Arnold Bennett continued to write fiction in this realist tradition and he was influenced by it. However, as his Bloomsbury colleague, Virginia Woolf, observed in an article published in 1927, such a detailed rendering of the social and material world was not enough for E.M. Forster. He was 'always constrained to build the cage – society in all its intricacy and triviality – before he can free the prisoner' (Virginia Woolf 'The Novels of E.M. Forster'). In an earlier paper called 'Mr Bennett and Mrs Brown' (1924), she made a distinction between Edwardian realists like Arnold Bennett, and a younger, more experimental generation of writers that she termed the Georgian **symbolists**. These included James Joyce, D.H. Lawrence – and E.M. Forster.

Clearly E.M. Forster draws on both conservative and innovatory techniques in his writing. He is less experimental, less radical in his novels than the younger generation of **Modernist** writers like Lawrence, Joyce and Virginia Woolf herself. He does, however, attempt to combine Edwardian realism with more exploratory techniques like **symbolism** in an effort to articulate more complex areas of individual experience and subjectivity. *A Passage to India* is the most Modernist of his novels. Published in the 1920s, it belongs with a group of texts, *Women in Love* (D.H. Lawrence, 1920), *The Waste Land* (T.S. Eliot, 1922), *Mrs Dalloway* (Virginia Woolf, 1925), that seek to make sense of a world traumatised by the First World War. It is less radical than they are, but shares some of their anxieties. It is in *A Passage to India* that E.M. Forster most questions his own values and exposes the limitations of his 'English' world view in the context of the challenging, foreign landscape and culture of the Indian sub-continent. But the time-setting of the novel is deliberately vague. E.M. Forster's second visit to India and the final drafting of the novel coincided with increasing activity for political independence, the Amritsar Massacre (1919), and Gandhi's passive resistance movement and imprisonment from 1922–4. However, such momentous events are only referred to obliquely in the text; E.M. Forster's primary concern is not political but metaphysical as he seeks to explore the limitations of language and meaning in an increasingly alien world.

# PART SIX

# CRITICAL HISTORY AND BROADER PERSPECTIVES

## RECEPTION AND EARLY CRITICAL VIEWS

*A Passage to India* was warmly received on its publication in 1924. The reviews were almost universally favourable and copies sold well on both sides of the Atlantic. Indian reviewers also felt that E.M. Forster had truthfully represented the political situation in India. The dissenting voices came from the Anglo-Indian community who felt that he had not been fair or accurate. In particular, Aziz's arrest and trial were felt to be a travesty of how such a case would be handled in actuality. There were stories of Anglo-Indians returning to India on their P. and O. liners throwing their copies overboard in disgust. Perhaps the most interesting contemporary response was from his fellow Bloomsbury Group member and rival novelist, Virginia Woolf. In her general appraisal of E.M. Forster's achievements in 1927 she wrote that his were 'a difficult family of gifts to persuade to live together' but his new work showed greater clarity of purpose. She concluded; 'it makes us wonder, What will he write next?' In the event, there were to be no more novels.

There are a selection of the early reviews in Philip Gardner's *E.M. Forster: The Critical Heritage* (Routledge and Kegan Paul, 1973). Virginia Woolf's article, 'The Novels of E.M. Forster', may be read there and in her *Collected Essays*, Vol 1 (Hogarth Press, 1966). Her earlier article, 'Mr Bennett and Mrs Brown' where she places E.M. Forster among the Georgian symbolists is also in this volume.

## LATER CRITICAL HISTORY

F.R. Leavis was the critic whose opinions carried most influence in English universities and schools in the years leading up to and beyond the Second World War. He constructed a **canon** of what he considered to be the greatest works of English fiction that he called 'The Great Tradition'. This was essentially a number of novelists who, he considered, celebrated the best values of nineteenth-century liberal civilization and criticised its worst, materialistic excesses. It began with Jane Austen and included

George Eliot, Henry James, Joseph Conrad and D.H. Lawrence. Interestingly E.M. Forster is denied a place in this 'Great Tradition' possibly because he was tainted by association with The Bloomsbury Group. Leavis was very hostile to the group, considering it to be a narrow, metropolitan coterie unrepresentative of English culture as a whole. No doubt E.M. Forster's slim output was also a disqualifying factor. However, Leavis did write approvingly of E.M. Forster, seeing in *A Passage to India* 'a more advanced maturity'. He singled out this novel as 'humane, decent and rational', 'a classic of the liberal spirit', and 'a most significant document of our age'.

The most influential critic of E.M. Forster's work in the immediate post-war era was the American Lional Trilling. He too saw E.M. Forster as a great spokesman for those liberal virtues of decency, tolerance and the principled private life for which America and Britain had fought fascism between 1939–45 and continued to fight communism during the Cold War. It was Trilling's book, *E.M. Forster* (Hogarth Press, 1944), that laid the foundation for E.M. Forster's steadily rising reputation in the 1950s and 1960s. He was the writer who asserted individual integrity against the encroaching power of mass movements and impersonal bureaucracies of all kinds. From this transatlantic viewpoint, E.M. Forster was seen as quintessentially 'English'. He was a writer of the Jane Austen school who 'refused to be great', a master of small-scale realism, irony, and self-deprecation. Later, it was another American, Frederick Crews, in his *E.M. Forster: the Perils of Humanism* (OUP, 1962), who saw *A Passage to India* as E.M. Forster's most revealing novel as it was India that exposed the limitations of this position.

The view of E.M. Forster as **realist** was modified by several critics who, taking the hint from E.M. Forster's own *Aspects of the Novel* (1927), began to stress the more **Modernist**, symbolic aspects of his texts. These include E.K. Brown's *Rhythm in the Novel* (University of Toronto Press, 1950), J. McConkey's *The Novels of E.M. Forster* (Cornell University Press, 1957), and some of the essays anthologised by Malcolm Bradbury in a collection of essays published in 1970. George Thomson in his *The Fiction of E.M. Forster* (Wayne State University Press, 1967), and Wilfred Stone in *The Cave and the Mountain* (OUP, 1966) took the debate into quite different areas. The former stressed the importance of myth and primitive religion; the latter also examined E.M. Forster's use of Jungian archetypes and symbols. Stone's book was particularly influential in the 1960s and neither treated E.M. Forster as primarily a novelist in the realist tradition.

A whole phase of E.M. Forster criticism came to an end with his death in 1970, the publication of his homosexual writings, and P.N. Furbank's massive *E.M. Forster: A Life* (Secker and Warburg, 1977–8). Drawing on hitherto unseen manuscript material, John Colmer's *E.M. Forster: The Personal Voice* (Routledge and Kegan Paul, 1975), can be seen as a work that draws together some of the representative strands in E.M. Forster criticism to that date, firmly placing his novels in their historical context.

F.R. Leavis's essay on E.M. Forster can be found in *The Common Pursuit*, first published in 1952 by Chatto & Windus, and reprinted many times since. Malcolm Bradbury's Macmillan Casebook on the novel (1970), contains much useful material up to that date including extracts from the interview E.M. Forster gave in 1952.

## SOME CONTEMPORARY APPROACHES

### DEVELOPMENTS IN CRITICISM SINCE E.M. FORSTER'S DEATH

The nature of the debate in literary studies has altered dramatically because of the interest in new literary theories since the 1970s. Now texts are often less valued for their qualities of formal organisation than for the contradictions and incompleteness that they display. Recent developments in both **Marxist** and **psychoanalytical** theory have stressed that texts are full of unresolved tensions and tangles as their authors struggle with social **ideology** or psychological repression. The more complicated these are, the richer the text is likely to be. According to one extreme view, texts owe their distinctive form more to the things they cannot say, than to the things that they do.

Another important development has been the interest in **Reader-Response** theory that focuses on how the reader makes meaning from a text, and how these meanings are, at least, partially determined by the reader's historical context and expectations. These, often unexamined, factors will effect how the reader responds to the challenges of a text and fills in those 'breaks' in the narrative that every fiction will have since it cannot cover every event exhaustively. All this is particularly relevant to any discussions of *A Passage to India*, since incompleteness, gaps in the text, muddle and confusion are a central feature of the text and E.M. Forster himself admitted that he 'didn't know' what went on in Adela's Marabar encounter.

Three recent approaches can be singled out as producing interesting, fresh work on this novel. They are listed separately, but, in practice, they often intertwine and merge together.

## POST-COLONIAL CRITICISM

The publication of Edward Said's influential *Orientalism* in 1978 (Penguin 1985) has led to a fresh appraisal of the manner in which the developed Western countries have historically represented the East in all the arts as well as a whole range of scientific and scholarly writings. It is Said's premise that the West has habitually dominated and controlled the East by making it 'Other'; that is, having qualities that make it separate and outside the norm of the civilised European centre. There has been an habitual, deeply ingrained need for the colonising powers of Western Europe to represent the East as mysterious, exotic, erotic, but also barbaric, superstitious and irrational. By this means, consciously or not, Imperial powers justify their occupation and seek to dominate and subdue their colonised or subservient peoples.

Because of this increased interest in the use of language as a means of power and control, it has become more difficult to see *A Passage to India* as a straight-forward attack on the authority of the British Raj. Post-colonial critics have shown that E.M. Forster's writing of India is implicated in his writing of 'Englishness'. His liberal position is not, and could not hope to be, disinterested. Despite his criticism of the Anglo-Indians, the 'real' India is as evasive as ever. It is marginalised, remote, not really seen. His Indian characters, Hamidullah, Mahmoud Ali, Aziz himself, are anglicised Indians with subservient roles in the administration of the Raj. Outside that narrow focus, all is strangeness, mystery and exoticism: for example, the water chestnut gatherer in Chapter 7 who understands Godbole's song, the beautiful impervious punkah wallah at the trial, and the child-like joy in the final ceremony at Mau. Moreover, in his suggestion of Mohurram unrest, the pillaging of goods at the station, Aziz's 'unreasonable' jealousy or in the inefficiency of India generally, E.M. Forster can be seen to be implicitly justifying the colonial rule that he seeks to criticise. Read in this light, the Marabar Hills epitomise the hostile non-European 'Other' that cannot be controlled or brought into order.

## FEMINISM

Feminism is now a broad school of criticism covering a wide range of approaches. *A Passage to India* has produced some interesting work from the post-colonial perspective. For example, it has been noted how all women, Indian and British alike, are marginalised in E.M. Forster's India. Hamidullah Begum may be in purdah, but so, in a sense, are Mrs Turton and Mrs Lesley at the Club. The imperialist world of Anglo-India is a very masculine affair where women are both publicly defended and privately resented. They are also powerless. Men negotiate and bond together using women, but actually ignore them. Adela's supposed assault in the Marabar Caves is the pretext for imperial brutality and the rallying cry to defend the 'women and children', but her distress is displaced onto Ronny. 'Bearing the sahib's cross' (Chapter 20, p. 175), he becomes the true victim. The caves expose gender exploitation as much as racial hatred. Rape and the fear of rape are used to silence and control women.

There is also a feminist line of argument that sees the 'extraordinary' Marabar Hills and Caves as an expression of the mothering body, repressed by **patriarchal** authority but still powerful. Seen in this light, the caves are a kind of womb and repository of female power; their disorientating echoes are the voice of the body unsettling the language of male culture and dominance.

## GENDER THEORY: THE WRITING OF SEXUALITY

E.M. Forster's sexual orientation had been more or less ignored until quite recently. Now, because of the interest in sexual politics and the ways in which writing is gendered, this has become an issue of more central critical concern. Undoubtedly part of the motivation for writing the novel was the appeal of an 'Orient' that had been highly, and ambiguously, sexualized in the Western mind. Viewed in this context, the yearning for the ideal 'Friend' in E.M. Forster's novel has a more erotic sense than might first appear. At the climax of the trial scene, not only does West view East through Adela's uncomprehending eyes, but female heterosexuality regards sexual 'Otherness' in the figure of the beautiful male punkah-wallah who presides over the proceedings.

Such readings of the novel focus on the friendship between Fielding and Aziz, noting how women mediate and frustrate male bonds generally. For example, the photograph of Aziz's dead wife helps to cement the relationship between the two men but Adela's accusation and subsequent withdrawal ensures its eventual failure. The Cave's 'ou-boum' hints at literarily 'unspeakable' desires that break up all socially acceptable relationships in the novel. From this perspective, the evasions and tenuous, inconclusive ending of *A Passage to India* have much to do with E.M. Forster's impatience with the conventions of **realism** which essentially support a heterosexual value system and a view of the world to which he cannot whole-heartedly subscribe.

Essays by Rustom Bharvcha, Benita Parry, Sara Suleri Goodyear, Brenda Silver and Penelope Pether collected by Jeremy Tambling for *E.M. Forster* (1995) in the Macmillan New Casebook series illustrate some of the new critical approaches taken to this novel. Also useful are *A Passage to India* (Theory in Practice Series, Open University Press, 1994) edited by Tony Davies and Nigel Wood, and an earlier collection of essays, *A Passage to India: Essays in Interpretation*, (Macmillan, 1985), edited by John Beer. There is an interesting chapter on the novel in Jennifer Sharpe's *Allegories of Empire: The Figure of Woman in the Colonial Text* (University of Minnesota Press, 1993). *E.M. Forster's India* (Macmillan, 1977) by G.K. Das provides valuable information on the colonial background to the novel. Benita Parry's *Delusions and Discoveries: Studies on India in the British Imagination, 1880–1930* (University of California Press, 1972) and Sari Suleri's *The Rhetoric of English India* (University of Chicago Press, 1992) explores issues of Imperialisn, culture and power, placing E.M. Forster's novel in a wider context of British writing about India. For gender theory, see also Joseph Bristow's chapter on the novel in *Effeminate England* (Open University Press, 1995); Alan

Sinfield's *The Wilde Century* (Cassell, 1994) gives earlier background information.

More generally, Barbara Rosecrance's *Forster's Narrative Vision* (Cornell University Press, 1982), has a detailed chapter on the language of the novel and Nicola Beauman's *Morgan: a Biography of E.M. Forster* (Hodder and Stoughton, 1993), is a recent study of his life. Finally, E.M. Forster's own writings are the best place to start any study of this novel especially his critical work, *Aspects of the Novel* (Edward Arnold, 1927) and the two collections of essays and reviews, *Abinger Harvest* (Edward Arnold, 1936) and *Two Cheers for Democracy* (Edward Arnold, 1951). *The Hill of Devi* (Edward Arnold, 1953) is a record of his own travels in India and provides an informative background to the 'Temple' section of the novel.

# CHRONOLOGY

| World events | Forster's life | Literary events |
|---|---|---|
| **1848** Revolutions in Europe | | |
| **1851** The Great Exhibition | | |
| **1857-8** Indian Mutiny - Indian forces massacre British residents at Lucknow, Delhi and elsewhere; revolt is crushed; the British assume full control of India | | |
| | | **1860** George Eliot, *The Mill on the Floss* |
| **1868** Gladstone becomes Liberal Prime Minister | | |
| **1869** Suez Canal is opened | | |
| **1870** Civil Service is opened to competitive examination | | |
| **1871** Paris Commune is suppressed | | **1871** George Eliot, *Middlemarch* |
| **1874** Disraeli becomes Conservative Prime Minister | | |
| **1877** Queen Victoria assumes title Empress of India | | |
| **1879** Gladstone denounces imperialism | **1879** Born in London on January 1 | |
| **1880** Gladstone becomes Prime Minister for the second time | **1880** His father dies | |
| | | **1881** Henry James, *The Portrait of a Lady* |
| **1885** The Indian National Congress is founded; The Labouchère Amendment to Criminal Law Act makes homosexual acts in private a crime | | |
| **1887** First Colonial Conference held in London | **1887** His great-aunt Marianne Thornton dies bequeathing him a legacy of £8000 | |
| **1892** Gladstone becomes Prime Minister for the third time | | |
| **1895** Oscar Wilde is tried and imprisoned | | |
| | **1897-1901** Undergraduate at King's College, Cambridge; elected to 'The Apostles' in his final year | |

| World events | Forster's life | Literary events |
|---|---|---|
| | | **1898** H.G. Wells, *The War of the Worlds* |
| **1901** Death of Queen Victoria | | |
| | | **1902** Arnold Bennett, *Anna of the Five Towns;* Henry James, *The Wings of a Dove;* Joseph Conrad, *Heart of Darkness* |
| | **1905** *When Angels Fear to Tread* | |
| **1906** Liberals achieve big victory at General Election | **1906** First meeting with Seyed Ross Masood | |
| | **1907** *The Longest Journey* | **1907** Joseph Conrad, *The Secret Agent* |
| | **1908** *A Room with a View* | |
| | **1910** *Howard's End* | |
| | **1911** *The Celestial Omnibus* | |
| | **1912-13** Visits his friend Massood in India and begins first draft of *A Passage to India* | **1913** John Maynard Keynes, *Indian Currency and Finance;* D.H. Lawrence, *Sons and Lovers* |
| | **1913-14** *Maurice* is written | |
| **1914-18** First World War | **1914** Forster travels to Egypt as a Red Cross worker | **1914** James Joyce, *Dubliners* |
| **1917** Russian Revolution | | |
| | | **1918** Lytton Strachey, *Eminent Victorians* |
| **1919** Amritsar Massacre in the Punjab - British forces kill more than 400 Indians and wound over 1200 | | |
| **1920-1** Gandhi introduces non-violent tactics in the Indian Independence movement | | **1920** D.H. Lawrence, *Women in Love* |
| **1921** Indian Central Legislature set up with limited powers | **1921-2** Visits India for a second time | |
| **1922-4** Gandhi is imprisoned | | **1922** T.S. Eliot, *The Waste Land;* James Joyce, *Ulysses* |

# CHRONOLOGY

| World events | Forster's life | Literary events |
|---|---|---|
| 1924 Labour Party takes office for the first time | 1924 *A Passage to India* | |
| 1926 General Strike in the UK | | 1926 Arnold Bennett, *The Clayhangar Family* |
| | 1927 Lectures in Cambridge on *Aspects of the Novel* | 1927 Virginia Woolf, *To the Lighthouse* |
| | 1928 *The Eternal Moment* | 1928 D.H. Lawrence, *Lady Chatterley's Lover* |
| 1930 Gandhi imprisoned for civil disobedience | | |
| 1931 Gandhi visits London to insist on all-India government | | |
| 1933 Hitler appointed Chancellor in Germany | | |
| | 1936 *Abinger Harvest* | 1936 John Maynard Keynes, *The General Theory of Employment, Interest and Money* |
| 1939-45 Second World War | | 1939 James Joyce, *Finnegans Wake* |
| 1945 Beginning of Cold War | 1945 Elected Honorary Fellow at King's College, Cambridge | |
| 1946 Hindu-Moslem riots in India | | |
| 1947 British India is divided into independent states of India and Pakistan; Nehru becomes India's first Prime Minister | | |
| 1948 Gandhi is assassinated | | |
| | 1951 *Two Cheers for Democracy;* writes the libretto for *Billy Budd* | |
| | 1953 *The Hill of Devi* | |
| 1960 Macmillan makes 'Wind of Change' speech | | |
| | 1970 Dies June 7 | |
| 1971 Bangladesh is formed | 1971 *Maurice* is published | |
| | 1972 *The Life to Come* is published – short stories written but unpublished throughout his life | |

SCALE in MILES
0          500

HIMALAYAS

Amritsar
Simla
Delhi
Jaipur
Indus
Ganges
Bankipore (1)
Lucknow
BARABAR HILLS (2)
CHHATARPUR (4)
DEWAS
Calcutta
Bombay
DECCAN PLATEAU (3)
Hyderabad
BAY of BENGAL
N
Bangalore
Calicut
INDIAN OCEAN

FICTIONAL NAMES for
PROPER LOCATIONS:-

1 Chandapore – Bankipore

2 MARABAR HILLS = BARABAR HILLS

3 DRAVIDIA = DECCAN PLATEAU

4 MAU = combined states of
CHHATARPUR & DEWAS

**anthropomorphism**  the attribution of human qualities to other living things or inanimate objects

**anticlimax**  deliberate descent from an elevated to low point often for comic effect

**canon**  in literary use, a selection of those works considered to be self-evidently of major significance

**closure**  the impression of completeness and finality at the end of a literary work

**coda**  a term from music indicating material added on that does not self-evidently belong to the main action

**comedy of manners**  a style of satirical comedy that examines the weaknesses and foibles of society

**dénouement**  the final unknotting of the plot

**dialogue**  directly reported speech and conversation of the characters in a literary work

**ellipsis**  the omission of words from the sentence

**eurocentric**  perceiving and judging the world from a European point of view

**feminism**  feminist criticism and scholarship seeks to explore or expose the masculine bias in texts and assert its own system of values

**free indirect style**  a technique of narrating the thoughts of characters that blends first and third person narrative. The effect is to be intimate and yet also detached

**hero, heroine**  the most important characters in a work of literature

**imagery**  the figurative language in a work of literature (metaphors and similes). Thematic imagery is that which recurs for a significant effect

**irony, ironic**  using words in a sense or context that implies the opposite meaning to what is actually said. Irony can also be situational. The writer shares with the reader or watcher information that the characters do not possess

**ideology**  the ideas, prejudices and value systems that exist in any society

**lacuna**  a gap, break or missing part of a text

**lyric, lyrical**  in a general sense, the yearning expression of an elevated mood or emotion

**marxism**  marxist criticism seeks to explore literature in the context of class struggle and economic injustice

**metaphor, metaphorical**  using language to identify one thing in terms of another

**modernism, modernist** in literary studies, a movement towards greater experimental forms of writing around and just after the First World War

**motif** a feature that recurs in a text for a deliberate artistic purpose. A **leitmotif** usually refers to this effect on a smaller scale like a repeated word or phrase.

**omniscient narrator** a story-teller who has a complete overview and control of the action

**Other, Otherness** as a noun, a term used in psychoanalytical criticism to refer to all that is not the self, usually in a threatening or challenging manner

**parody** a mocking copy of something serious

**patriarchal** term used in feminist criticism to refer to a system of value and control dominated by men

**persona** a mask used to project the writer's personality through another character

**personify, personification** giving human qualities to inanimate objects

**plot** the plan of a literary work involving a pattern of relationships and a chain of events linked by causation

**point of view** the perspective or position from which the reader experiences the events in a text

**psychoanalytical** psychoanalytical criticism explores the creative process and attempts to explain literature using models drawn from the theories of the unconscious and the human mind

**realism, realist** a term usually used to refer to fictions written in the nineteenth century that depict an explicable social world full of lively comprehensible characters with firm narrative control. Such fictions have interesting, complicated plots and a satisfying ending

**reader-response** reader-response criticism focuses on the relationship between the reader and the text, and the processes by which the reader makes sense of the text and interprets it

**satire, satirical** holding up folly or vice to ridicule

**simile** describing one thing in terms of another by making the point of comparison obvious

**symbol, symbolic, symbolist** investing objects in the material world with the suggestive power of abstract, complex ideas

**theme** the abstract subject of a work. A central idea behind its composition

Nigel Messenger was educated at St Luke's College, Exeter and the University of Leicester. He has co-edited a volume of minor Victorian poetry and written books on E.M. Forster and D.H. Lawrence. He is a Senior Lecturer at Oxford Brookes University, where he lectures on Victorian and early Modern literature. He is the author of the York Notes Advanced on *Great Expectations*.

## GCSE and equivalent levels (£3.50 each)

Maya Angelou
*I Know Why the Caged Bird Sings*

Jane Austen
*Pride and Prejudice*

Alan Ayckbourn
*Absent Friends*

Elizabeth Barrett Browning
*Selected Poems*

Robert Bolt
*A Man for All Seasons*

Harold Brighouse
*Hobson's Choice*

Charlotte Brontë
*Jane Eyre*

Emily Brontë
*Wuthering Heights*

Shelagh Delaney
*A Taste of Honey*

Charles Dickens
*David Copperfield*

Charles Dickens
*Great Expectations*

Charles Dickens
*Hard Times*

Charles Dickens
*Oliver Twist*

Roddy Doyle
*Paddy Clarke Ha Ha Ha*

George Eliot
*Silas Marner*

George Eliot
*The Mill on the Floss*

William Golding
*Lord of the Flies*

Oliver Goldsmith
*She Stoops To Conquer*

Willis Hall
*The Long and the Short and the Tall*

Thomas Hardy
*Far from the Madding Crowd*

Thomas Hardy
*The Mayor of Casterbridge*

Thomas Hardy
*Tess of the d'Urbervilles*

Thomas Hardy
*The Withered Arm and other Wessex Tales*

L.P. Hartley
*The Go-Between*

Seamus Heaney
*Selected Poems*

Susan Hill
*I'm the King of the Castle*

Barry Hines
*A Kestrel for a Knave*

Louise Lawrence
*Children of the Dust*

Harper Lee
*To Kill a Mockingbird*

Laurie Lee
*Cider with Rosie*

Arthur Miller
*The Crucible*

Arthur Miller
*A View from the Bridge*

Robert O'Brien
*Z for Zachariah*

Frank O'Connor
*My Oedipus Complex and other stories*

George Orwell
*Animal Farm*

J.B. Priestley
*An Inspector Calls*

Willy Russell
*Educating Rita*

Willy Russell
*Our Day Out*

J.D. Salinger
*The Catcher in the Rye*

William Shakespeare
*Henry IV Part 1*

William Shakespeare
*Henry V*

William Shakespeare
*Julius Caesar*

William Shakespeare
*Macbeth*

William Shakespeare
*The Merchant of Venice*

William Shakespeare
*A Midsummer Night's Dream*

William Shakespeare
*Much Ado About Nothing*

William Shakespeare
*Romeo and Juliet*

William Shakespeare
*The Tempest*

William Shakespeare
*Twelfth Night*

George Bernard Shaw
*Pygmalion*

Mary Shelley
*Frankenstein*

R.C. Sherriff
*Journey's End*

Rukshana Smith
*Salt on the snow*

John Steinbeck
*Of Mice and Men*

Robert Louis Stevenson
*Dr Jekyll and Mr Hyde*

Jonathan Swift
*Gulliver's Travels*

Robert Swindells
*Daz 4 Zoe*

Mildred D. Taylor
*Roll of Thunder, Hear My Cry*

Mark Twain
*Huckleberry Finn*

James Watson
*Talking in Whispers*

William Wordsworth
*Selected Poems*

*A Choice of Poets*

*Mystery Stories of the Nineteenth Century including The Signalman*

*Nineteenth Century Short Stories*

*Poetry of the First World War*

*Six Women Poets*

## York Notes Advanced (£3.99 each)

Margaret Atwood
*The Handmaid's Tale*

Jane Austen
*Mansfield Park* ·

Jane Austen
*Persuasion*

Jane Austen
*Pride and Prejudice*

Alan Bennett
*Talking Heads*

William Blake
*Songs of Innocence and of Experience*

Charlotte Brontë
*Jane Eyre*

Emily Brontë
*Wuthering Heights*

Geoffrey Chaucer
*The Franklin's Tale*

Geoffrey Chaucer
*General Prologue to the Canterbury Tales*

Geoffrey Chaucer
*The Wife of Bath's Prologue and Tale*

Joseph Conrad
*Heart of Darkness*

Charles Dickens
*Great Expectations*

John Donne
*Selected Poems*

George Eliot
*The Mill on the Floss*

F. Scott Fitzgerald
*The Great Gatsby*

E.M. Forster
*A Passage to India*

Brian Friel
*Translations*

Thomas Hardy
*The Mayor of Casterbridge*

Thomas Hardy
*Tess of the d'Urbervilles*

Seamus Heaney
*Selected Poems from Opened Ground*

Nathaniel Hawthorne
*The Scarlet Letter*

James Joyce
*Dubliners*

John Keats
*Selected Poems*

Christopher Marlowe
*Doctor Faustus*

Arthur Miller
*Death of a Salesman*

Toni Morrison
*Beloved*

William Shakespeare
*Antony and Cleopatra*

William Shakespeare
*As You Like It*

William Shakespeare
*Hamlet*

William Shakespeare
*King Lear*

William Shakespeare
*Measure for Measure*

William Shakespeare
*The Merchant of Venice*

William Shakespeare
*Much Ado About Nothing*

William Shakespeare
*Othello*

William Shakespeare
*Romeo and Juliet*

William Shakespeare
*The Tempest*

William Shakespeare
*The Winter's Tale*

Mary Shelley
*Frankenstein*

Alice Walker
*The Color Purple*

Oscar Wilde
*The Importance of Being Earnest*

Tennessee Williams
*A Streetcar Named Desire*

John Webster
*The Duchess of Malfi*

W.B. Yeats
*Selected Poems*